Adva

"Johnson's unrivaled knowledge of South Sudan's history is apparent throughout this concise and readable book. His approach is both sympathetic and critical: South Sudan's current woes are explicable, but not inevitable. It would be easy to see South Sudan's history simply as a bleak story of oppression and misrule; but Johnson shows us that it is also a story of innovation and courage. South Sudan has a deeply problematic historical legacy, and the current situation is dire: yet as this timely book shows, it is not hopeless."

—Justin Willis, coeditor of *The Sudan Handbook*

"It is a challenging intellectual responsibility to write a 'new history for a new nation,' but it is difficult to imagine anyone better qualified to do it than Douglas Johnson. In this brief book Johnson not only covers the entire sweep of the history of southern Sudan from the ancient period to the present day but evokes with precision and nuance crucial developments in the history of region and nation and its peoples."

—Charles H. Ambler, author of *Kenyan Communities in the Age of Imperialism*

"*South Sudan: A New History for a New Nation* is the best current political history of the world's youngest nation by its most prominent living historian."

—Deborah Scroggins, author of *Emma's War*

South Sudan

OHIO SHORT HISTORIES OF AFRICA

This series of Ohio Short Histories of Africa is meant for those who are looking for a brief but lively introduction to a wide range of topics in African history, politics, and biography, written by some of the leading experts in their fields.

South Sudan

A New History for a New Nation

Douglas H. Johnson

OHIO UNIVERSITY PRESS

ATHENS

Ohio University Press, Athens, Ohio 45701
ohioswallow.com
© 2016 by Ohio University Press
All rights reserved

Printed in the United States of America
Ohio University Press books are printed on acid-free paper ⊗ ™

26 25 24 23 22 21 20 19 18 17 16   5 4 3 2 1

Cover design by Joey Hi-Fi

Library of Congress Cataloging-in-Publication Data
available upon request

For Wendy, with love

Contents

Illustrations

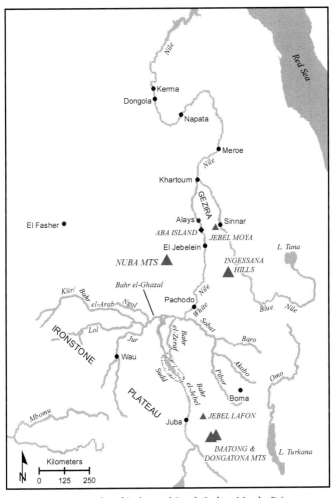

Map 1 Topography of Sudan and South Sudan. *Map by Brian Edward Balsley, GISP*

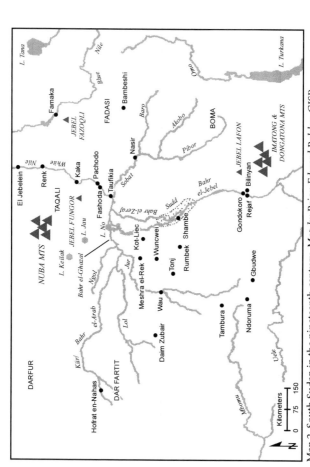

Map 2 South Sudan in the nineteenth century. *Map by Brian Edward Balsley, GISP*

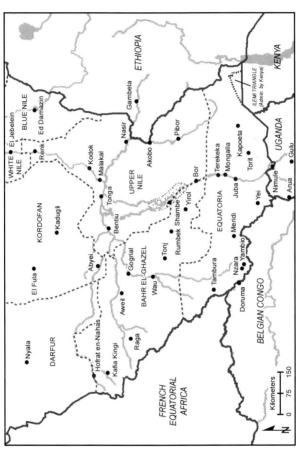

Map 3 South Sudan in 1956. *Map by Brian Edward Balsley, GISP*

Map 4 South Sudan in 2011. *Map by Brian Edward Balsley, GISP*

1

Introduction

"This Is Where We Came From"

On 9 July 2011 I attended South Sudan's formal independence ceremony in Juba, an event that marked a departure for Africa. Most African countries became independent on a negotiated "transfer of power" from a colonial authority to a new national elite. South Sudan's independence came from the directly expressed will of its people. There was a shared sense of the historical importance of the event beyond the exercise of self-determination by Africa's newest nation. My companions that day included a Kenyan and a Ugandan, both from communities who shared languages and histories with South Sudan. "This is where we came from," one of them commented. "This is our home."

Watching the arrival of several African heads of state, one sensed a change in Africa as well. When the Organization of African Unity (OAU) was founded in the early 1960s, Sudan was already locked in its first civil war. South Sudan's exile leaders, fighting what they called their own anticolonial struggle, were shunned

15

by the new African governments bound in solidarity to each other. South Sudanese warnings against the nascent OAU becoming a club for dictators proved all too prescient, but as John Garang, South Sudan's leader in the second civil war, later commented, "We were the pariahs of Africa," and the warnings were ignored. Yet here Africa's leaders now were lining up to watch the flag of one African Union member go down as that of a future member went up.

My own introduction to South Sudan began more than forty years earlier as a student at Makerere University College in Uganda sharing classes with South Sudanese refugee students. Sudan was then nearing a turning point in its long first civil war. Ja'afar Nimeiri's May Revolution had proclaimed that the war needed a political rather than a military solution. Southern guerrilla forces, the Anyanya (named after a local poison), were finally coalescing around a unified leadership. Despite pronouncements of an imminent peace, the war continued for nearly three more years.

This was also a time of revolution in the writing and teaching of African history, moving beyond the histories of colonial pioneers and embracing the investigation of the indigenous past. The recently published *Zamani: A Survey of East African History* presented an integrated regional history based on this new research. As welcome as this was, there were still some silences. East Africa stopped at the northern borders of Uganda and Kenya. Aside from references to prehistoric "River

Lakes Nilotes" and nineteenth-century "Khartoumers," South Sudanese history was absent. I came away from these combined experiences with the desire to write for South Sudan the type of history that now defined the field of African history.

I was fortunate to be able to begin substantive research inside South Sudan during the period of the Addis Ababa peace between 1972 and 1983, and to observe the evolution of historical research through alternating periods of peace and war. Prior to 1972 the main focus had been on the causes of civil war (e.g., Oduho and Deng 1963; Beshir 1968; Abdel-Rahim 1969; Albino 1970; Wai 1973). The outlines of South Sudan's long colonial period were delineated in the pioneering works of Richard Gray (1961), Robert Collins (1962, 1968, 1971, 1983), and the Sandersons (1981). While virtually no one claimed as bluntly as A. J. Arkell that South Sudan had no history before 1820, the year of Egypt's invasion of Sudan (Arkell 1961, 2), the internal histories of South Sudanese societies received little attention during the Addis Ababa peace when new fieldwork was possible. The long second civil war refocused attention on the twin tragedies of war and slavery (Wakason 1984; Hutchinson 1995; Jok 2001; Beswick 2004). The conclusion of peace in 2005 reopened South Sudan to field-based research, and a new generation of researchers has continued the work of earlier field-workers in creatively combining exploration literature, administrative records, and older ethnography with new fieldwork (e.g., Jal 1987; Simonse 1992; Leonardi 2013a; Cormack 2014; Tuttle 2014; Stringham 2016). There is now also a serious effort to examine South Sudanese intellectual history and the ideas underpinning its nationalist ideology (Poggo 2009; Tounsel 2015), as well as detailed studies of the conduct, consequences, and aftermath of war (Schomerus and Allen 2010; LeRiche and Arnold 2012; Pinaud 2013; Badiey 2014; Grabska 2014; Falge 2016).

A new history of South Sudan thus has much to draw on. There are still many challenges, quite apart from the basic contradiction here of attempting to fit a *longue durée* history into a Short History series. There are lingering stereotypes in the earlier literature commonly referred to and promoted by South Sudanese themselves that must be confronted. Because the historiography of South Sudan has lagged behind much of the rest of Africa's, the quality of the sources and the way they have been used must be examined. For this reason there will be a running reference to historiography throughout this text. Inevitably chapters become more detailed the closer we get to the present, but they will not be detailed enough for those readers who are mainly interested in what is happening now. The purpose of a longue durée history is to give shape to a nation's past and not let the present define that past.

Ever since Richard Gray's characterization of southern Sudan as isolated from the great centers of power and historical trends of the continent (Gray 1961, 8–9), writers have taken the region's historical isolation as proven, even describing the region as "cut off from the rest of the world" and "as remote an environment as can be found" (LeRiche and Arnold 2012, 4; cf. Poggo 2009, 21). But representatives of nearly every major African language group are found within its borders. One of the themes of this book is to show how South Sudan is a missing piece in the jigsaw puzzle of African history and identify both historic and recent connections between South Sudanese and communities beyond their borders. A new history for a new nation must combine the internal history of indigenous communities with a record of South Sudan's involvement with the wider region.

Writers have also found the complex ethnic makeup of South Sudan a challenge to describe. Embarrassed by the colonial overtones of the word "tribe," they replace it with either "ethnic group" or "clan," implying that all South Sudanese societies are bounded by small kin-based groups. There are serious objections to using "tribe" in any context (Ehret 2002, 7), but "tribe" and "ethnic group" are not interchangeable. Anthropologists Ferguson and Whitehead make a useful distinction between tribes as "bounded and/or structured political organizations" and ethnic groups, which "are a cultural phenomenon with only latent organizational potential" (2000, 15). In South Sudan's ethnographic and administrative literature "tribe" and "clan" have distinct meanings and are not interchangeable. Tribal organizations are recognized administrative units with their own internal political structure: the Nuer people are organized into a number of different tribes, as are the Dinka people. Clans are kin units whose significance differs among South Sudan's many peoples: some are territorial and central to a tribe's political organization, others are nonterritorial and widely dispersed. In this book I use the word "people" to describe groups who share the same language and similar social principles or cultural practices, "tribe" when referring to specific administrative-political units, and "clan" only when appropriate for certain kin groups. The use of ethnic names in South Sudan is undergoing a change as South Sudanese intellectuals seek to replace the English terms with indigenous self-names. However, until some consensus is reached I retain the more conventional forms established in the literature: Shilluk rather than Collo or Ocolo, Nuer rather than Naath, Dinka rather than Jieng, Mandari rather than Mundari, Lotuho rather than Otuho, and so on.

Linguistic terms are sometimes applied as broad ethnic labels, and there are also popular meanings unrelated to scholarly use. The term "Nilotic" is particularly problematic. Linguists now identify three broad branches of Nilotic within the Nilo-Saharan language family: Western, Eastern, and Southern (see chapter 2). The first are found in Ethiopia, South Sudan, and Uganda; the second in South Sudan, Uganda, and Kenya; and the last in Kenya and Tanzania. Yet "Nilotic" also has different cultural and political connotations. In Ethiopia it is a general term for lowland peoples of diverse languages and origins. In Uganda it refers to the peoples of the north associated with past dictatorial regimes, not all of whom speak a Nilotic language. It has acquired similar political overtones in South Sudan and is applied almost exclusively to the Western Nilotic-speaking Nuer, Dinka, and Shilluk, less often to the Atuot and Anuak, but not to the Mabaan, Acholi, and Pari. I use it here only in its linguistic sense. The Eastern Nilotic languages of Bari, Lotuho, Toposa, Turkana, and Maasai were at one time classed as "Nilo-Hamitic" but, as the "Hamitic hypothesis" of a race of light-skinned civilizers in African history has been thoroughly discredited and we now recognize that there were no such people as "Hamites," there can be no merging of Nilotes with Hamites, and the archaic label "Nilo-Hamitic" has been dropped even by linguists.

Religion is another area of confusion. Despite the existence of a large body of sophisticated ethnographic descriptions of South Sudanese spiritual beliefs, the great majority of South Sudanese are routinely dismissed as "animists" who worship spirits embedded in natural objects. The anthropologist E. E. Evans-Pritchard explicitly stated that the Nuer "are not animists and there is no evidence that they ever have been" (1956, 158), yet journalists still write of them as praying to their "animist gods" (Purvis 1993, 46). Animism has no place in the description of African religions, for as Chris Ehret trenchantly states, "This terminology, besides failing to fit any particular African religion, does violence to historical reality: it lumps in an amorphous mass what are in actuality immensely different sets of ideas with distinctive consequences for the history of thought and culture in different parts of the continent" (2002, 15). South Sudan has a long history of the mingling of monotheistic ideas and theistic religions, both indigenous and imported.

Terms of indigenous authority in South Sudan also vary according to ethnographic tradition, alternating between kings and chiefs. Here I follow the anthropologist Simon Simonse's useful restatement of the distinction between the two. Kingship is not determined by the size of territory over which authority is claimed but by the exercise of sovereignty over a whole structure. A chief is a subordinate in that structure, "a local-level official whose authority depends on a long-standing connection with his subjects and on recognition by a more powerful state" (Simonse 1992, 7). By this definition there were many kingdoms in precolonial southern Sudan, but the basis on which a king exercised sovereignty differed between societies.

The sources for the study of South Sudan's past vary in quality. The archaeological record has not got beyond the exploratory stage. Historical linguistics is providing avenues for making long-term connections between significant language groups, but a thorough analysis of Western and Eastern Nilotic is yet to be completed. For the nineteenth century there is a wealth of contemporary observations in the exploration literature, sources of primary importance but ethnographically superficial and inaccurate (Evans-Pritchard 1971b, 145). The administrative literature of the first half of the twentieth century provides a more intimate contemporary record, especially in the local documents being assembled in the South Sudan National Archive, as it was produced by men conversant in some of the languages of South Sudan and in long-term contact with its peoples. Yet as detailed as these documents are they still provide mainly an external view of South Sudanese peoples and their societies. We are fortunate to have an extensive body of contemporary field-based ethnographic literature created by anthropologists such as Evans-Pritchard, Godfrey Lienhardt, and Jean Buxton and by missionary ethnographers and linguists such as Fathers Hofmayr, Crazzolara, and Santandrea, which helps us understand how South Sudanese peoples organized themselves, interacted with their environment and each other, and responded to internal and external events to become the peoples they are today. The writing of South Sudan's history must build on this ethnographic foundation as new fieldwork begins a more systematic collection of South Sudanese oral testimony.

African historians have developed tools for analyzing oral sources, but these have not been systematically applied in South Sudan. There is a need to establish reliable, if relative chronologies. The narratives of population migrations are told in foreshortened time, compressing multiple movements and a complex series of attachments and separations into a single strand. The standard method of counting the generations backward from the present to a founding ancestor is unreliable because the purpose of tribal genealogies is not to measure time but to establish social and political connections. As the anthropologist Ian Cunnison warned, "Historically a tribal genealogy is, purely and simply, a falsification of the record" (1971, 189). Nuer and Dinka genealogies express both social and political distance within and between lineages rather than time depth (Evans-Pritchard 1940a, 107–8, 198–99; Lienhardt 1958, 106). Establishing any dates much beyond five generations on the basis of genealogies without first analyzing indigenous systems of time reckoning and age-sets is speculative, and recent valiant attempts to extend tribal chronologies backward into a medieval past are yet to be confirmed (e.g., Beswick 2004; Kuendit 2010).

Dynastic lists, such as those of the Zande and Shilluk kings and the Dinka spear-masters, offer another approach to chronology. Of these, the Shilluk king list has been the most studied and begins to give us semireliable dates for events along the White Nile, especially when corroborated by the dynastic lists of the Blue Nile sultanate of Sinnar. But even dynastic lists are problematic. The king lists for the Ugandan kingdoms of Buganda and Bunyoro, for instance, expanded in the twentieth century as clan ancestors and clan shrines were incorporated in the genealogies as a way of enhancing dynastic prestige through the assertion of greater antiquity (Henige 1980). The Shilluk king lists vary between sources, many disputed kings are included, and regnal dates are calculated in different ways (Westermann 1970, 135; Hofmayr 1925, 48; Howell and Thompson 1946, 84; Crazzolara 1951, 135–38; Lwong 2013). What can be said with some certainty is that the kingdom was well established by the early to mid-seventeenth century, and that with the founding of the royal capital at Pachodo toward the end of that century, the installation of the *reths* (kings) became institutionalized and more reliable dating can proceed from that time.

In any book of the longue durée there is the danger of reading back into the past identities that were centuries in the making. With South Sudanese still debating their own national identity, it would be an anomaly to apply the terms South Sudan or South Sudanese to earlier periods. At the risk of offending South Sudanese readers, I will refer to southern Sudan and southern Sudanese for periods before the mid-twentieth century and to South Sudan and South Sudanese when describing the evolution of nationalist politics. I will use the administrative terms of Upper Nile, Bahr el-Ghazal, and Equatoria where convenient, even though the composition of those regions changed over time (the Zande kingdoms, for instance, at different times were part of Bahr el-Ghazal, Equatoria, and Western Equatoria).

Themes of violence and war run throughout this book, but there are other aspects of the shared experience of South Sudanese that have promoted co-existence in the past and might be the foundation for reconstruction in the future. Ancestral southern Sudanese societies were part of a Sudanic culture with other Nile Basin communities and drew on a common pool of symbols, images, religious ideas, and patterns of authority. Modern South Sudanese societies are products of a long process of cultural assimilation and borrowing of ideas and institutions between communities.

Mobility and migration are common themes through several historical periods. South Sudan is a mosaic of settled agricultural communities, centralized states, and mobile nonstate pastoralist societies. States fostered assimilation of different peoples, often by force. Nonstate societies provided an alternative to states, even for northern Muslim pastoralists who sought refuge among Nilotic border communities to escape the demands of the northern sultanates.

South Sudan has experienced an escalation of violence ever since the intrusion of external powers in the nineteenth century. New technologies of war brought new forms of military and political organization. The Turco-Egyptian conquest of Sudan radically altered relations between many southern Sudanese communities and between southern Sudanese and their northern neighbors. The wars of the twentieth and twenty-first centuries were greater in scale than the wars of the nineteenth not only in their levels of violence, the involvement of external powers, and their impact on civilian communities but in their legacies of violence during subsequent periods of peace.

Warfare on an expanded scale accelerated population dispersal and the formation of new communities through the recombination of scattered peoples. The introduction of slavery and the international slave trade created the new phenomenon of south Sudanese diasporas, exported to other parts of Sudan and beyond, or combined into the military formations of multiple armies. The refugee diasporas produced by Sudan's postindependence civil wars have been scattered across the globe. They are now returning, as earlier diasporas did, with acquired experiences and skills that will have a significant impact in shaping South Sudan's future.

The experience of multiple colonialisms defined the territorial and political outlines of South Sudan and helped shape the definition of who was South Sudanese. The trade empires of the nineteenth century shifted regional connections and created networks that began to knit together the different territories of southern Sudan. The dual colonialism of the twentieth-century Anglo-Egyptian Condominium, where Sudan remained an Egyptian colony governed by Britain, left a contradictory legacy. Local administration was established by force but is remembered as benign in the creation of an administrative system based on customary law and customary institutions, though neglectful of education and economic development under the restricted terms of the Southern Policy.

The history of Sudan and South Sudan since the mid-twentieth century is a history of contested nationalisms and the failure of the politics of national unity. The power struggle between the northern nationalist parties left the southern provinces and other rural regions marginalized from the centers of economic and political power. The emergent South Sudanese political elite began to fashion a coherent nationalist ideology of its own, based mainly on opposition to the northern parties' construction of a national identity around the external ideologies of pan-Arabism and Islamism. South Sudan's struggle was and continues to be part of a wider struggle in postindependence Sudan, a struggle that remains unresolved by South Sudan's own independence referendum. The failure of the politics of national unity in Sudan has contributed to the current failure of the politics of national unity in South Sudan.

There is as yet no single comprehensive history of South Sudan, and this short history can be no more than an introduction to some basic facts, ideas, and interpretations, illustrated by vignettes of specific persons or events. It cannot name-check all the peoples of South Sudan or do justice to all their historical traditions. It is offered to stimulate conversation, debate, and further research about South Sudan's past. All historical writing is a work in progress, and this book is no more than an interim report.

2

South Sudan in the Nile Basin

In 1929 a German tourist reading a local paper on the verandah of Khartoum's Grand Hotel was surprised by a story about the recently destroyed "Pyramid of Dengkurs" in the village of the "wizard" Guek Ngundeng. Having viewed the remains of the step pyramids at Meroe and declared them debased African versions of Egyptian prototypes, his imagination raced backward and forward in time. "A pyramid!" he exclaimed. "What pyramid? Who has been buried there, thousands of years ago: demigod, priest, or Ethiopian king? And wizards? What sorcery are they practicing, what is this, what is still living there in those impenetrable swamps?" (Bermann 1931, 19).

This encounter illustrates how the history of Sudan has often been obscured by the assumptions of Egyptology. Influences flowed in one direction from the Egyptian heartland, and a conical mud shrine in the "impenetrable swamps" of the Upper Nile could only be understood as a degenerate pyramid. Yet, as the archaeologist David Wengrow reminds us, the ancient civilizations of the Nile Valley and Near East "were the products of interaction and exchange, rather than isolation." They were "the outcome of mixtures and borrowings, often of quite arbitrary things, but always on a prodigious scale" (2010, 13, 175). Recent advances in archaeology and historical linguistics now recognize that ancient Egypt, rather than being the source of all invention, often built on innovations originating further up the Nile. Exchanges and borrowings flowed both down- and upriver between the Nile's African heartland and the civilizations along its middle and lower reaches, contributing to the spread of a shared pool of cultural ideas and practices from which Nile Basin societies drew, however distant from each other in time or space. The peoples of southern Sudan, whose geographical, political, and cultural isolation from the rest of Africa is commonly assumed, were active participants in these exchanges and interactions.

Nilo-Saharan Populations

Most South Sudanese belong to the Nilo-Saharan language family, the bearers of the ancient Sudanic civilization that originated in the Middle Nile, stretching from the Niger bend to the Red Sea coast. In the differentiation of languages and the movement of populations through and beyond the Sudanic belt over several millennia, Nilo-Saharan peoples "drew on a common fund of basic ideas about politics, social relations, and religion" (Ehret 2001a, 224).

The homeland of the ancestral Nilo-Saharan speakers straddled the two Niles from their confluence southward to Lake No. The two primary branches of Koman and Sudanic began to emerge some thirteen thousand years ago. The modern representatives of Koman include today's Gumuz, Uduk, and Koma located along the Sudan-Ethiopian borderlands, close to their ancestral homeland. The more numerous Sudanic branch is further subdivided into Central and Northern subbranches. The modern representatives of Central Sudanic include the Bongo and the so-called Fartit (Yulu, Kresh, Aja, Golo, and so on) of the Bahr el-Ghazal basin, and the Moru, Madi, and Lugbara in the present-day South Sudan–Uganda borderlands. The modern representatives of Northern Sudanic are more widely spread geographically and more divergent linguistically. They include the Nubian languages of the Sudan-Egyptian border, Fur and Daju in Darfur, many of the languages of the Nuba Mountains, Gâmk in the Ingessana hills of Blue Nile, Surmic speakers of southwest Ethiopia and southeast South Sudan (Murle, Didinga, Larim, and Mursi), the Western Nilotes (Dinka, Nuer, Atuot, Shilluk, Anuak, Mabaan, Acholi, and Pari), Eastern Nilotes (Bari, Mandari, Lotuho, Lokoya, Toposa, Jiye, Nyangatom in South Sudan, and Turkana and Maasai in Kenya), and the Southern Nilotes of Eastern Africa (Ehret 2001b).

Geographically South Sudan connects East Africa's Great Lakes to the sahelian steppe of Sudan. Topographically it is an "irregularly shaped basin," elevated around its perimeters, drained in the west by the rivers

Table 2.1 Some languages of South Sudanese and related peoples

NILO-SAHARAN PEOPLES
  KOMAN
    Uduk, Komo, Gumuz
  SUDANIC
    CENTRAL SUDANIC
      Mangbetu, Moru, Madi, Lugbara, Bongo, Fartit, Aja,
      Kresh, Baka
    NORTHERN SUDANIC
      Fur
      EASTERN SAHELIAN
        Nubian
        Daju
          Nyalgulgule
        Jebel
          Gâmk
        Surmic
          Murle, Didinga, Larim, Mursi, Tirma
        Nilotic
          Western Nilotic
            Jii (Dinka, Nuer, Atuot)
            Luo (Shilluk, Anuak, Pari, Acholi)
            Mabaan
          Eastern Nilotic
            Bari, Mandari
            Ateker (Turkana, Toposa, Jiye, Nyangatom)
            Maa (Maasai, Lotuho, Lokoya)
          Southern Nilotic
            Kalenjin
NIGER-CONGO PEOPLES
  ADAMAWA AND UBANGIAN
    Zande, Nzakara, Ndogo, Sere, Mondu, Mangaya,
    Bai, Bviri
  BANTU
    Homa

of the Nile-Congo watershed and in the east by the So-bat-Pibor system, both converging on the main channel of the Nile and the central *sudd* swamp. South Sudan's soils are broadly divided into alluvial clays and heavy loams in the east, and lighter laterite soils of the iron-stone plateau in the west. The alluvial clays, found in the former provinces of Upper Nile and Jonglei, parts of Eastern and Central Equatoria, and much of Bahr el-Ghazal, are high in nutrients and covered by tall grass and woodlands, beneath which lie South Sudan's known oil reserves. The eastern clay plains are flat, with almost no slope, and are prone to waterlogging in the rains and cracking in the dry season. Permanent settlements are possible only on a few slightly elevated sandy ridges. The ironstone plateau covers most of the former provinces of Bahr el-Ghazal, and Western and Central Equatoria. Its soils are better drained than the clays, with lower nutrients, covered by broad-leafed woodlands and forests, and able to support larger populations in permanent settlements (SDIT 1955, 3–4).

Average yearly rainfall increases along a north-south axis, with much drier conditions experienced along the northern border with Sudan. With its higher rainfall, its network of waterways, its waterlogging clay soils and central swamp, the southern Sudan has always been a wetter region than the northern territories of the Middle Nile, a factor influencing long-term population movements. In the wetter conditions throughout northeast Africa approximately twelve to five thousand years ago, the central swamp and the pattern of seasonal flooding covered a greater area and extended farther north than today, and this is one reason why the area was settled later than the central Nile Valley. Drier conditions began to set in some five thousand years ago, and it is likely during this period that previously inaccessible areas of the region were populated, contributing to the differentiation between languages and social groups (Harvey 1982, 14–17).

The first peoples to spread south of the Bahr el-Ghazal flood basin were the Central Sudanic–speaking societies, with the Bongo and so-called Fartit speakers settling south of the Bahr el-Ghazal and the ancestral Moru, Madi, and Lugbara speakers reaching the northwestern part of the East African Rift. About four thousand years ago the ancestral Nilotic speakers began moving south from the eastern Middle Nile Basin as the central sudd swamp began to shrink. During the last millennium BCE the Western Nilotes separated into ancestral Dinka, Nuer, and Luo as they spread throughout the region between the two Niles; the Eastern Nilotes settling in the central Equatoria region began to diverge into ancestral Bari, Toposa, and Lotuho-speaking communities; and the ancestral Didinga-Murle entered the area of southwestern Ethiopia and southeastern southern Sudan (Ehret 1982, 22–27; 2001a, 247; 2002, 126, 388). From the thirteenth through the nineteenth centuries CE there were further movements of Western Nilotic-speaking societies around, through, and out of the central swamp region as new and hardier breeds of cattle were introduced, allowing for longer-range movement (David 1982a, 54–55; 1982b, 86–88).

This compressed chronological summary might give the impression of large-scale population movements of whole peoples over a relatively short time, but the linguistic evidence reveals "a complex array of human interactions, involving often the extensive amalgamation of people from formerly separate societies" (Ehret 1982, 34), as the next chapter describes.

Sudanic Civilization, Sacred Bulls, and Symbols of Power

The Sudanic Civilization emerging out of the Nilo-Saharan tradition along the middle Nile between eleven and eight thousand years ago had a number of distinctive features. These included the domestication of cattle and indigenous wild grains such as sorghum, and the creation of a pottery tradition some two thousand years before similar developments in the Middle East. A parallel aquatic tradition, recalled in the fishing spear (*bith*) so symbolically important in modern Nilotic religions, involved the intensification of hunting and gathering riverine resources along the expansive networks of rivers and major lakes. A cluster of monotheistic ideas developed around a single divinity associated with the sky, rain, and lightning (the antithesis of "animism") and the emergence of sacral chiefship or kingship where both the office and the person of the king were associated with divinity but where the king was not divine (Ehret 2001a; 2002, 61–94).

The dominant cultural features that gave the early Neolithic Nile Valley its distinctive character came from its "primary pastoral communities." During the fifth millennium BCE human populations from Sudan's Gezira to the Nile Delta developed a mobile pastoralism of mixed herds and shared materials and ritual practices, some originating in Sudan before appearing in Egypt. Herding mobility created a pattern of social and cultural integration, which allowed for internal variations that were later accelerated by the intensification of stockbreeding as a mode of livelihood (Wengrow 2003, 133–34; Wengrow et al. 2014).

During this early period we see the beginnings of the "bovine idiom" common to various Nile Basin societies in different epochs. Training the horns of display cattle into different formations has been practiced along the Nile from Neolithic times through the Egyptian Old Kingdom and the kingdoms of Kerma and Meroe (Wengrow 2006, 56; Welsby 1996, 154) to present-day South Sudanese pastoralists (Evans-Pritchard 1940a, 45; Lienhardt 1961, 16–17; Buxton 1973, 7). Cattle burials are also a practice of some antiquity. Cattle have been found buried in early Neolithic cemeteries in middle Egypt and central Sudan, sometimes within human burials, sometimes separately (Wengrow 2003, 128; 2006, 56–59). Ox skulls and whole ox skeletons have been found in royal tombs and other important gravesites in Nubia, Kerma, and Meroe (Adams 1977, 157, 197, 407; Welsby 1996, 91). The sacred Apis Bulls in dynastic Egypt had their own burial rites. In more recent times cattle in southern Sudan have also been slaughtered and buried in the foundations of shrines, as with Ngundeng Bong's Mound (the "Pyramid of Dengkurs") among the Nuer, constructed in the 1890s (Johnson 1990, 53–54; 1994, 93).

Cattle burials point to the continued ritual importance of cattle among herding societies from Neolithic times in Egypt to present-day South Sudanese pastoral communities, and this, rather than some fanciful "pyramid" within the swamps, is the real point of comparison between ancient and modern societies. Insofar as modern pastoral communities have shared interests in cattle, the sacrifice of cattle becomes an "affirmation of community interests" (Lienhardt 1975, 229), an interpretation that might apply to the ritual importance of cattle burials involving sacrifice in the past. Religious shrines among Western Nilotic–speaking pastoralists are often constructed as cattle barns (*luak*), and even large conical mound shrines built of mud imitate this shape and are referred to as luaks (Howell 1948, 1961; Mawson 1989; Johnson 1990). Some Dinka extend the sacred image to a primordial past by claiming that their ancestors originated in the "luak of creation" (F. Deng 1980, 251). But even when detached from an association with fixed shrines, cattle become "wandering shrines" when dedicated to specific divinities (Evans-Pritchard 1940a, 209).

The points of comparison go beyond the physical treatment of cattle in life or death and are found in the symbolism associated with the divine. The Nuer often refer to divinity by the "poetic epithet" of Tutgar, an ox-name derived from a majestic bull with wide, spreading horns, sometimes represented as holding the universe or the earth between them (Evans-Pritchard 1956, 4). Like Tutgar, the sacred Apis Bull of New Kingdom Egypt was also often depicted with spreading horns embracing not the earth, but the sun. The comparison between Tutgar and the Apis Bull goes beyond horn formations and takes us directly to the Sudanic religious color symbolism associated with divinity, the sky, rain, and lightning.

The Apis Bulls were black with a white mark on their heads, said to be conceived by a lightning bolt and to have the image of an eagle on their backs. These symbolic associations with the divine are part of the cluster of ideas expressed in ancestral Sudanic religions and are found in many modern South Sudanese societies. Lightning is associated with divinity. The combination of black and white colors in cattle as well as in birds and other animals evokes the image of rain and rain clouds, also associated with divinity. Dinka and Nuer name an animal with a white head and black (or dark) body after the fish-eagle (*kuei*) because of its similar black and white markings (Lienhardt 1961, 11–14, 162; Evans-Pritchard 1940a, 41; 1956, 31–32, 53–54, 81; Buxton 1973, 6–7, 385).

In the color symbolism of South Sudanese cattle keepers the alternating pattern of light and dark is evocative of rain clouds, lightning in a dark sky, or stars in the night, all manifestations of divinity in one form or another (Lienhardt 1961, 12; B. Lewis 1972, 49; Buxton 1973, 385). Just as a black bull with a white head is named after the fish-eagle, so a spotted beast will be named after the leopard (*kuac*), and leopard skins have had royal or priestly associations as emblems of authority not only in ancient Egypt, which imported leopard skins from lands further south (Trigger 1976, 39, 56, 111; Baines 1995, 120; Williams 1997) but among such modern South Sudanese communities as the Dinka, Nuer, Anuak, and Acholi (Bedri 1948, 50, 57; Evans-Pritchard 1940a and 1956; Crazzolara 1953, 11; Lienhardt 1975, 224–26).

Recent interpretations of archaeological and historical evidence now suggest that the kingdoms of the Middle Nile were built on the foundations of the Sudanic Civilization and that, far from being replications of the Egyptian Pharonic model, the Nubian kingdoms of Kerma, Napata, and Meroe were early examples of Sudanic states (Edwards 1998, 2003; Fuller 2003; Ehret 2001a, 240–42, 245; 2002, 92–94, 149). These multiethnic, polyglot kingdoms with multiple centers of power derived their position more by gaining social influence over people than by absolute control over territory, a building of "wealth in people" that was later replicated in southern Sudan. The territories of Napata and Meroe extended just south of the confluence of the Niles, into the northern fringes of the proto-Nilotic homeland, with pastoralist groups located both within the state's heartland and along and just beyond its periphery. Both states and nonstate peoples shared essentially the same systems of production, and the two lived in symbiotic tension as states attempted to expand relationships of power built on exchange, trade, and local alliances. It was through the ancient trading networks of the Nile Valley that valuable commodities from the peripheries, including animal skins with their symbolic value, found their way north, and it was through the economic means of trade that the relatively powerful Middle Nile states attempted to exert their influence over peripheral societies—patterns later repeated in recent times (James 1977, 107–8). To what extent the activities of the early Sudanic states contributed to the southward movements and internal differentiation of the proto-Nilotic-speaking societies has yet to be determined.

Forms of Sudanic sacral chiefship or kingship were practiced by states and by nonstate peoples. Among Western Nilotes both kings and sacral chiefs are associated with divine power. The Shilluk reth is seized by the spirit of the first reth, Nyikang, upon his installation (Howell 1953). The sacral chiefs of the Dinka, Atuot, and Nuer are imbued with *ring*—the priestly divinity Flesh (Lienhardt 1961, 135–46, 172, 227–30; Burton 1987, 84–85; Johnson 1994, 57–59). The human sacrifice associated with the burial of early Sudanic kings developed into socially sanctioned regicide in the country of the two Niles, where the king was not allowed to die a natural death lest the spiritual power inherent in the institution be diminished. Regicide was practiced not only among the Shilluk but also in the territory of the kingdom of Sinnar, once widely populated by Western Nilotic Luo speakers related to the Shilluk (Evans-Pritchard 1932, 60–61), and among many Dinka groups who bury alive their sacral chiefs, the *bany bith* spear masters (Lienhardt 1961, chap. 8). The Eastern Nilotes of Equatoria also practice regicide, dispatching their rainmaker kings in times of drought (Simonse 1992, chap. 17 and conclusion; Angok 2015).

It is important to reemphasize the point that the foregoing comparisons do not establish a direct unbroken relationship between modern and ancient Nile Basin societies (Wengrow 2003, 132). What they do establish is that Nile Basin peoples have been drawing on a common pool of ideas and symbols in a variety of ways over several millennia, often reinforced by two-way exchanges between societies of unequal power. They also further undermine the assertion of South Sudanese cultural isolation and reestablish South Sudan's place within the broader range of African history.

3

Trees and Wandering Bulls

Describing the environment of southern Sudan in the 1870s, the nineteenth-century naturalist Georg Schwein-furth declared, "It has been a land without chalk or stone, so that no permanent buildings could be constructed; it has consequently reared a people which have been without chiefs, without traditions, without history" (1874a, 145). Neither traditions nor history are confined to permanent buildings, and what the naturalist overlooked was that southern Sudanese had numerous natural landmarks on which to construct both tradition and history.

A large tamarind tree used to stand in the western Nuer village of Kot-Liec in what is now Unity State. Many Nuer myths identify it as the place where the ancestors of the Nuer and other peoples first appeared. Even though the original tree no longer exists, the site is still sacred, a place for offerings and sacrifices (Crazzolara 1953, 8–9, 66–68). For some Nuer, stories of their historically datable migrations begin with the tree at Kot-Liec. A Gaawar man described how the Gaawar ancestors came down from the sky to settle in the west "one by one," just as their people later crossed the river to settle in the east "bit by bit" (Johnson 1994, 50–51). One twentieth-century Nuer prophet even described it as "the cradle of the human race. Mohammed El Rasul (Prophet Mohammed), Kerek (Kerec tribe [the Baggara], Bel (Jur Bel tribe), Kutet (Shilluk tribe), Kunuar (Nuer) and Jang (Dinka tribe) were born and dispersed at 'Liic'" (Ruei Kuic quoted in Johnson 1994, 312).

The reconstruction of the internal history of South Sudanese societies must analyze such indigenous accounts. Considered simultaneously as myths and legends, they contain both religious and historical explanations about their societies (Lienhardt 1975, 213–14). Recurring motifs found across many South Sudanese societies include ancestral trees, lost spears, stolen beads, and wandering bulls. Set in an unspecified past, these stories offer distilled versions of historical experience rather than a factual record of events. In addition to explaining the origins of societies, they explain processes of incorporation, differentiation, separation, and migration.

Stories of Separation and Migration

Trees are associated with founding ancestors in origin stories or are commemorated as clan divinities among many communities. Large shade trees such as the tamarind (*Tamarindus indicus*) and fig (*Ficus sycomorus* and *Ficus platyphylla*) often figure in this way. As such these trees are communal symbols, symbols of communities past, present, and future, and are seen as creating communities by gathering people under and around them.

Stories of trees are sometimes combined with the myth of a rope connecting the earth and the sky. The rope and the tree were the means by which humans descended to earth and returned to the sky to be rejuvenated when old. Cutting the rope or destroying the tree, preventing humans from returning to the sky, is a religious explanation for the separation of humankind from divinity and for the permanence of death. But the cutting of the rope or the destruction of the tree also evokes historical experiences of how communities are created as well as divided.

Among the Nuer the tamarind tree is a symbol of social and genealogical incorporation, where ancestors were brought into the community on earth and retained, a mythological representation of the Nuer practice of incorporating foreigners into their lineage system (Johnson 1994, 45). Elsewhere the severing of the rope or the cutting down of the tree explains not incorporation but separation and loss. Among the Eastern Nilotic Mandari, a quarrel between the people on the earth and in the sky, or between Mandari clans, results in the severing of the rope and people separating (Buxton 1963, 20–25). Among the Koman-speaking Uduk and Western Nilotic Mabaan of the Ethiopian foothills, the mythical tree has the Western Nilotic–sounding name "Birapinya," echoing the Western Nilotic imperative for "come down," for instance, *biä piny* in Shilluk and *bir piny* in Nuer. Its destruction has a more poignant ending. The tree is burned and people are stranded in the sky, all except those who are able to carry others on their backs as they jump down to earth. Caught between powerful kingdoms along the Sudan-Ethiopian borderland as they were, the Uduk have had the historical experience of being scattered by raiders: survival depended on mutual protection in common flight, but survivors lost all contact with those left behind (James 1979, 68–73). The Mandari and Uduk might have borrowed details of the myth from Western Nilotes, but they refashioned the themes to express different historical experiences. Yet the association of the tree with separation is found even among the Western Nilotic Jo-Luo of Bahr el-Ghazal. They locate the historical division between the ancestors of two major Luo groups at Wuncwei, "the place of the tamarind tree," northeast of Tonj (Santandrea 1968, 114–15, 160–61).

There are other explanations for segmentation and separation more rooted in everyday experience than in a mythical connection with the sky. A recurring motif repeated among the Jo-Luo, Shilluk, Anuak, Dinka, and Nuer; the Lotuho, Pari, and Bari of Equatoria; and even the Alur and Acholi of Uganda is the story of the lost spear and the stolen bead. The common theme is the breach of relations between neighbors or relatives. A borrowed spear is lost and the owner insists on the return of the exact same spear rather than its replacement, forcing the borrower to go to extreme lengths to retrieve it. The child of the spear's owner is accused of swallowing a bead belonging to the borrower, who

45

retaliates by insisting on the return of the exact same bead and the evisceration of the child. Because of these acts the groups of the two protagonists are unable to live together and part company (Lienhardt 1975, 221–33).

The story is repeated in so many versions among so many societies over such a large area that it cannot, of course, be attributed to a historical event. It accounts, for instance, for the separation of Nyikang and Dimo, the founders of the respective Shilluk and Anuak royal dynasties, that some say took place at Wuncwei. As with the myths of the tree, the interpretation of the symbolism varies. For the Nilotic kingdoms—the Shilluk, Pari, Anuak, Acholi, Alur, and Lotuho—the myth represents dynastic politics, the spear and the bead becoming royal emblems with one branch of the royal house attempting to absorb or destroy the other. For the Dinka and Nuer, the sequence of events threatens to upset the balanced system of exchanges on which their segmentary political systems depend, alternating between the extremes of total assimilation of one group by another and total separation (Lienhardt 1975). For others, such as the Lokoya and Lopit in Equatoria, it accounts for the separation of related groups (Simonse 1992, 53, 303–6). Among the Bari the story explains the origin of a taboo between two clans (Beaton 1936, 114–15).

The myths of the spear and the bead may be schematic versions of the historical experiences of dynastic rivalries or segmentary opposition, but there is a moral point that is of broader relevance to all communities within South Sudan today. In his analysis of these myths the anthropologist Godfrey Lienhardt pointed out that "the common moral theme is obviously that getting your very own back, a kind of reciprocation without exchange, leads to the permanent alienation of neighbours so that they can never again live together as members of the same community" (1975, 216).

There are other remembered causes of separation and migration that might in fact be rooted in historical events, though told in stereotypic forms. Given the importance of primary pastoral communities in the ancient history of the Nile Valley mentioned in chapter 2, it is not surprising that the peopling of the Nile Basin is often attributed to people following their cattle. Wandering bulls, thematically the opposite of trees as fixed points of communal origin, have had an actual as well as a mythical role in history.

Fights between bulls of the same or neighboring herds are commonly recalled as the reason for lineages splitting up and moving apart, or for establishing the seniority of one chiefship over another (Evans-Pritchard 1940a, 33–34; F. Deng 1980, 269–70). They even figure in the foundation myths of kingdoms, and the founding of two royal capitals are attributed to wandering cattle. The first Funj king of what became the Muslim sultanate of Sinnar is said to have followed a bull from his home on Jebel Moya to the site of his new capital on the Blue Nile (Holt 1973, 76). Similarly Reth Tugo of the Shilluk followed his favorite hornless ox (*cod* in Shilluk) to the site near the White Nile that became known as Pachodo (Fashoda), "the village of the hornless ox" (Westermann 1970, 138). The Ngok Dinka adapted the Sinnar founding myth to explain their own migration from the region between the Niles to the Ngol river in what is now the disputed Abyei region between Sudan and South Sudan (F. Deng 1980, 256). Of these stories, probably only the founding of Pachodo can be considered historically true and datable to the end of the seventeenth century, but they are consistent not only with what we know of the transhumant patterns of movement of all cattle keepers in the Nile Basin but of the gradual penetration of southern Sudan by pastoral communities during the transition from wetter to drier periods.

There are links to be made between different stories of migration, but weaving them all into one grand narrative has produced varying results. The closeness of the different Luo languages in eastern Africa suggests a very recent spreading of peoples and languages, but attempts to locate a Luo cradle land from different versions of the spear and the bead stories have produced no consensus. Father J. P. Crazzolara, who worked among Luo speakers in the southern Sudan and northern Uganda, located his cradle land along the border of the two countries. The Kenyan Luo historian B. A. Ogot placed his cradle land firmly in Kenya, while Evans-Pritchard and Simon Simonse, working in eastern Equatoria, postulated a Luo homeland there (Crazzolara 1951; Ogot 1967; Simonse 1992, 56–57). Tracing the itineraries of the Luo migrations through southern Sudan, the Great Lakes, and East Africa does at least highlight southern Sudan's engagement with, rather than isolation from, neighboring regions and is why, for instance, a Kenyan Luo guest at the independence celebrations could say, "This is our home." The itineraries are not necessarily only mythical. The Pari, an offshoot of the Anuak, established a route from lowland Ethiopia to Jebel Lafon in eastern Equatoria several centuries ago. It was through this route that they acted as middlemen in precolonial trade between western Ethiopia and the equatorial Nile, expanding their links in the nineteenth century to include the Great Lakes (Kurimoto 1995). The Sudan People's Liberation Army (SPLA) later followed this same route when infiltrating eastern Equatoria from its Ethiopian bases in the 1980s.

The main historical point to emphasize here is that stories of migration do not tell the whole story, and possibly not even the most important story. People move, but not necessarily all at once. A people can expand its population and territory through the incorporation of smaller groups, through intermarriage, and through the adoption of individuals. Ethnic identity is not fixed; a person from one group can become a member of another. The clan histories of the Anuak, Pari, Bari, and Mandari, among others, record many with foreign origins (Evans-Pritchard 1940b, 31–33; Simonse 1992, 54–56; Buxton 1963, 18–19, 32–33; Leonardi 2013a, 22), and a number of Shilluk clan names are shared

49

with more distant peoples (Westermann 1970, 128–33; Crazzolara 1951, 156–59; 1954, 391–92). Languages also spread, sometimes farther and faster than people. As Noel Stringham acutely observes, "'Nilotic migrations' had more to do with people changing who they were than where they were" (2016, chap. 1). The Western Nilotic words for village or territory, *pa* and *pan,* are found in a variety of forms (*fa/fam/fan,* and possibly *ba/bam/ban*) well beyond the current area inhabited by Western Nilotes: Fanyar in Kordofan, Basham in White Nile, Fazoqli and Bani Mayu in Blue Nile, and Bambashi, Fadasi, and Famaka in western Ethiopia. Mabaan is currently classed as a Western Nilotic language related to Shilluk, Dinka, and Nuer, yet the Mabaan are socially and culturally closer to their Koman-speaking Uduk neighbors (they are both matrilineal) than to the nearest Western Nilotic speakers (who are all patrilineal). The as yet unanswered question is: Are the Mabaan an offshoot of the ancestral Western Nilotes who were influenced by the surrounding Koman people, or are they Koman-speakers who adopted a Western Nilotic language? And could the answer be: a bit of both?

There have been many other types of reciprocal influences and borrowing between language communities. The Luo-speaking Pari and Acholi of eastern Equatoria, along with the Anuak of the Sobat-Pibor system, might at one time have formed a near-continuous band of Luo peoples before becoming separated from each other by, and intermingled with, Eastern Nilotic (Bari and Lotuho)-, Central Sudanic (Madi)-, and Surma (Murle and Didinga)-speaking groups. "Far from being a collection of neatly arranged, different ethnic communities each with its own language, culture and migration history," Simonse proposes, "the east bank of the Nile proves an area where processes of cultural assimilation between various groups of peoples have gone on for a considerable period of time" (1992, 50–59). Chief among these exchanges have been age-class systems and forms of kingship.

The peoples of eastern Equatoria have complex and sophisticated systems of age-classes and age-grades, unlike age-sets among the Dinka and Nuer that established a loose hierarchy of generations creating social solidarity between men of a specific age-range, provided a limited structure for the exercise of political power by older age-sets over younger ones, and created a basic military organization whereby age-mates joined together when called on to fight. But both the political and the military roles were minor, there was no formal progression of age-sets from junior to elder status, and there were no rites for the transfer of authority. The *monyomiji* age-class system that originated among the Lotuho involved more structured age-grading in the allocation of military and political tasks within a society and a more formal advance from one stage in a generation's life to the next. It has been adopted and adapted by many other Eastern Nilotic communities, including Lokoya and the eastern Bari, but also by the Central

Sudanic Madi-speaking Lolubo, the Surma-speaking Tenet, and the Luo-speaking Pari and Acholi (Simonse 1992, 46–47; 1998, 52; Kurimoto 1998).

States and Antistates

Southern Sudanese peoples have been described as living in "pristine anarchy" (Collins 1962)—archetypical models of stateless societies, totally unprepared for their encounter with powerful states to the north (Gray 1961, 8–9). There was in fact a more dynamic set of power relations along what is now the borderland between South Sudan and Sudan. From the sixteenth century through to the mid-nineteenth century this region was dominated by a series of kingdoms: the Funj Sultanate of Sinnar on the Blue Nile, the Shilluk Kingdom on the White Nile, the Kingdom of Taqali in the Nuba Mountains, and the Darfur Sultanate in the west. A network of nonstate southern Sudanese societies along the waterways flowing into the White Nile both challenged and contained contemporary states, even offering sanctuary to refugees from state demands. The cultural, social, and political distance between the peoples of what are now known as two different countries was then very narrow. Further south other nonstate peoples lived sometimes in opposition to and sometimes in symbiosis with a variety of kingdoms.

The kingdoms of Sinnar, Shilluk, and Taqali shared many characteristics of their population and their royal customs. The founding of the Sinnar sultanate might

have been part of a Nubian revival, but some historical traditions credit the Shilluk with either founding
the sultanate or contributing greatly to its expansion
(O'Fahey and Spaulding 1974, 24–26). The populations
of both the Funj and Shilluk kingdoms included many
peoples indigenous to the region along and between
the two Niles: Koman, Nuba, Luo, and other Western
Nilotes, among others. In all three kingdoms royal succession depended on the support of the maternal kin of
the new king (Lienhardt 1955, 29–30; Ewald 1990, 68–
69; O'Fahey and Spaulding 1974, 46). The Nuba of Jebel
Fungor are classificatory "sister's sons" to the Shilluk
reths through an ancient marriage into the royal clan
and continue to play a role in the investiture of each new
reth (Lienhardt 1955, 35; Howell and Thompson 1946,
38; Ewald 1990, 36).

A number of royal systems devolved from the separation of the Shilluk and Anuak, represented above as
resulting from a quarrel between two founding kings,
Nyikang and Dimo. Each of these systems displayed
some aspect of sacral kingship mentioned in chapter 2. In
both the Shilluk on the White Nile and the Anuak along
the Sobat-Pibor system, kingship descends through a
single clan (Lienhardt 1955, 30–31). No Shilluk reth
can reign until formally installed at Pachodo, where the
spirit of Nyikang enters his body. The reth is not allowed
to die a normal death, being either assassinated by a
rival or "helped" to die when ill. The Anuak kingship is
more symbolic than political and is determined by the

possession of certain royal regalia, whose transmission was often decided by regicide (Evans-Pritchard 1940b, 87). In eastern Equatoria kings (Acholi *rwot* and Pari *rwath*) were often associated with rainmaking, and there are also Luo rainmaking clans among the Bari, Lulubo, and Madi (Simonse 1992, 54–56).

A far different form of kingship was introduced by the Azande from the Mbomu river system in what is now the Central African Republic. Their kingdoms were organized around families of Avongara aristocrats who created assimilationist states, built on the strength of converting subject peoples into servants of the king and the court as conscripts into the king's regiments and as cultivators enabling the king to amass surpluses of food for redistribution. Internal justice was maintained through the kings' monopoly of a type of poison obtained in long-distance trade and used as an oracle to determine guilt or innocence in life-or-death issues. The Azande began moving out from between the Mbomu and Shinko rivers in the first half of the eighteenth century, entering the Nile-Congo watershed region around the beginning of the nineteenth. A king's son would be given his own frontier province, and the princes expanded their holdings or created new kingdoms by destabilizing and conquering their neighbors. The terror the disciplined Zande regiments inspired was enhanced by their reputation—whether deserved or not—of being cannibals, a reputation physically reinforced by the practice of filing their teeth to sharp points. Conquest brought assimilation, and the Zande language spread as the kingdoms incorporated communities originally speaking Sudanic, Bantu, and Nilotic languages throughout territories now contained within the Central African Republic, the Democratic Republic of Congo, and South Sudan (Evans-Pritchard 1971a, 23–25, 269–78).

The most powerful kingdoms and states had a severe impact on their neighbors. Both the sultanates of Sinnar and Darfur were slave-raiding states, making regular forays into the hills of the Blue Nile hinterland, the White Nile plain, and the forests of western Bahr el-Ghazal. Along the White Nile the Shilluk countered and even at times checked the advances of Sinnar through fleets of canoe-borne raiders (Mercer 1971). An alternative to all these states was provided by the Padang Dinka.

The Padang Dinka tribes (including the Abialang, Paloich, and Dungjol on the White Nile and the Rueng and Ngok along the Bahr el-Ghazal and Kiir/ Bahr el-Arab systems), being segmentary societies, had an ability to form social alliances across communities and developed as antistates, providing alternatives for peoples fleeing state authority. The Abialang, Paloich, and Dungjol established themselves on the east bank of the White Nile throughout the seventeenth century and by around 1775 had decisively defeated the forces of Sinnar as far north as present-day Renk and Jebelein (Westermann 1970, lv; Hofmayr 1925, 66–68;

Bedri 1948, 40–42; O'Fahey and Spaulding 1974, 61–63, 98). Farther west, Rueng sections dominated the grazing areas between the Bahr el-Ghazal and lakes Keilak and Jau/Abiad, while the Ngok Dinka settled along the Ngol and Kiir/Bahr el-Arab rivers toward the end of the first half of the eighteenth century, assisting the Humr Baggara Arabs in clearing the area of its original inhabitants and offering refuge to both the Rizeigat and Humr Baggara when they fled the demands of the sultan of Darfur (El-Tounsy 1845, 129–30; Henderson 1939, 58–59, 61–64, 76; O'Fahey 1980, 99). By the beginning of the nineteenth century the main powers along the northern waterways were not the Muslim sultanates of Sinnar and Darfur but the states and antistates of the Shilluk, Anuak, and Dinka.

4

Trade and Empires, Tribal Zones and Deep Rurals

The former slave Salem Wilson recalled witnessing raids conducted by well-armed miniature armies against villagers armed only with bows and spears. "We need not dwell on the attack," he wrote, "I have too vivid a recollection of the reality," but he was explicit about the fate of the survivors. "We leave the slain and the dying, and watch the treatment dealt out to the poor prisoners. . . . The men are yoked with leather thongs to long poles, and their hands tied behind them. They then load the poor women with what have heretofore been their household goods, and make them carry these like beasts of burden" (1901, 25). Describing the aftermath of such raids, Evans-Pritchard later observed, "The tribes of the Bahr-el-Ghazal present the appearance of a routed army" (1931, 15). The military image was apt. The Turco-Egyptian state's reliance on armed commerce in its southward expansion brought about a massive change in power relations and population distribution within southern Sudan. The military forces of state agents, trading companies, and their armed allies created new power centers that had a direct impact on indigenous social and political systems.

From the 1820s up to 1840 southern Sudanese contact with the expanding state was confined mainly to the Shilluk and Dinka between the two Niles. During the next two decades more areas in the interior were opened up to river-borne trade as government flotillas and trading companies expanded into the southern waterways. In the 1860s power shifted to the commercial companies as their private armies spread through the *zariba* system, a network of fortified trading stations. Commerce was founded on the trade in ivory and slaves, the latter seized in warfare, and relations between traders and southern Sudanese, in Richard Gray's telling phrase, descended into a "vicious spiral of violence" (1961, 54).

Egypt attempted to assert its control over indigenous peoples and merchant companies alike, recruiting a succession of European administrators in the 1870s and 1880s ostensibly to expand government authority, suppress the slave trade, and support legitimate commerce. The power of the traders was broken by 1879, but the methods and even the personnel of the Egyptian administration scarcely differed from that of the traders as government troops occupied the same sites and continued to plunder local peoples for food, supplies, and captives. The outbreak of the Mahdiyya in the 1880s precipitated a rapid collapse of the Egyptian administration in its southern provinces, but the Mahdists were unable to retain control of more than a few river ports, from which they sent out raiding parties until expelled from the region by Belgian, French, and Anglo-Egyptian forces in the late 1890s. Patterns established in the nineteenth century continued well into the twentieth.[1]

Tribal Zones and Deep Rurals

The early colonial history of southern Sudan is an example of expanding states creating "tribal zones" along their peripheries through trade and war. Progressive militarization transformed indigenous social relations, political structures, and patterns of warfare, leading to wars of resistance, panethnic alliances, ethnic soldiering with indigenous peoples fighting on the side of or under the control of the expanding state, and internecine wars to control trade or seize plunder (Ferguson and Whitehead 2000).

But there is a parallel process in response to encroaching commercial networks of the sort that southern Sudanese experienced in the nineteenth century. The accepted picture of southern Sudan at this time is one of relentless destruction, a "rape of the Sudd" with whole communities defenseless against the onslaught of foreign exploiters. As Cherry Leonardi has pointed out, this is only part of the story, and the nineteenth century was also a time of engagement and adaptation by many southern Sudanese societies (2013a, chap. 1). We can understand this period better through the anthropological concept of "deep rurals," a term first applied to West Africa to describe the ambivalent relationship between market centers and peripheral agricultural communities. To maintain their autonomy within regional systems created and dominated by plantations and markets, deep rural communities adopt a number of strategies, including selective trading with markets, absorbing runaways and debtors, and living symbiotically with more mobile pastoralists (Jedrej 1995; James 2015).

The late nineteenth-century history of southern Sudan illustrates these related processes. Foreign state presence constantly redefined itself, first facilitating the activities of commercial companies, then subduing them and grafting government administration onto the network of trade centers and caravan routes the companies had created, before giving way to the militant Mahdist theocracy operating through a much reduced network. Indigenous communities, too, alternated between accommodation with and resistance to the new powers in the land. Communities living in close proximity to the new military-commercial centers became captured labor, while other communities adopted deep rural strategies to maintain their autonomy.

The Rape of the Sudd and Patterns of Authority

At the beginning of the nineteenth century each of the Sudanic states had their own tribal zones. The Tunisian traveler and scholar Muhammad al-Tunisi identified them as the lands of enslaveable peoples: the Nuba south of Sinnar and the Fartit south of Darfur. Neither Nuba nor Fartit were specific ethnic labels, but expressed the combination of ideas about religion and ethnicity that defined the categories of "free" versus "slave," who could raid and who could be raided (O'Fahey 1982, 77; Ewald 1990, 48). It is significant that al-Tunisi's list did not explicitly mention the Shilluk and Dinka. Before Egypt's invasion of Sudan, both peoples were as often raiders as raided. By the end of the nineteenth century, however, the whole of southern Sudan had become a tribal zone of the old Turco-Egyptian empire followed by the advancing Anglo-Egyptian state.

For some two centuries the Shilluk dominated the White Nile, using canoes to raid Baggara cattle keepers and downstream Muslim villages, and alternately taxing or disrupting trade where the east-west trade routes crossed their territory. By the end of the eighteenth century Aba Island was a Shilluk island and the river from Alays to Kaka was known to neighboring Arabs as "Bahr Shilluk," the river of the Shilluk (Mercer 1971, 407–18).

Armored cavalry were at the core of the armies of Sinnar and Darfur, but they were of little use against canoe-borne raiders. Nor did they have a marked edge over Dinka spearmen, who developed their own tactics to neutralize cavalry's advantage, as the Turco-Egyptian army learned to its cost in its first foray into the White Nile plains in 1827 (Bartoli 1970, 7–8, 34–35). In the west the formal cavalry-mounted slave raids launched from Darfur into the forested valleys of western Bahr el-Ghazal had become a stylized form of warfare during the first half of the nineteenth century, aimed at increasingly scattered communities of Fartit rather than the stronger Malual Dinka who, together with the Ngok Dinka to the east, controlled most of the river Kiir, the geographically misnamed Bahr el-Arab (O'Fahey 1980, 93–94). Despite often being in conflict with these demographically strong Shilluk and Dinka societies, the Sinnar sultanate and the Baggara also often sought them as allies (Hofmayr 1925, 66–68; Henderson 1939, 63–64; O'Fahey 1980, 99).

The Turco-Egyptian invasion of Sudan in 1820 disrupted these local balances of power. The viceroy of Egypt, Muhammad Ali, sought to secure gold and slaves for his army with which to challenge the overlordship of the Ottoman sultan. The failure to find both in sufficient quantities did not lessen the impact on the peoples from Nubia to Sinnar who were subject to new forms of land tenure and taxation. With these new demands came new opportunities. Slave raiding, slave trading, and slave owning had been state activities in Sinnar and Darfur, but Egypt's demand for taxes to be paid in slaves enabled northern peoples such as the Shaiqiya and the pastoralist Rufa'a and Baggara to participate in government slave raids, paying their taxes in captured slaves and keeping the surplus. After Egyptian flotillas opened up the Nile tributaries south of the Shilluk to commerce in the 1840s, hard-pressed Nubian peasants found a way not just to escape debt but to acquire wealth through employment in the trading companies that soon entered southern Sudan searching first for ivory and then for slaves (Spaulding 1982; Bjørkelo 1989).

The opening of the upper Nile basin to both commerce and slave raiding was made possible when Egypt wrested control of the White Nile from the Shilluk by siting shipbuilding yards along the river to construct the wooden sailing boats that could carry large numbers of armed men and large amounts of cargo. Aba Island was still described as a Shilluk island in the mid-1850s, but the Shilluk lost control of the area in the early 1860s (Mercer 1971, 412, 418; Taylor 1970, 328, 332–33; Petherick 1869, 89–90). The timber of the well-forested island attracted shipbuilders from Nubia, among them a Dongolawi carpenter, Muhammad Ahmad, who in the 1880s would proclaim himself the Mahdi and launch his rebellion against Egypt from his island base.

The erosion of Shilluk power was a decades-long process. The Shilluk kingdom had consolidated its strength in the late eighteenth and early nineteenth centuries during the life of its long-reigning reth, Nyakwac, but began to lose control during the reign of his son Nyidhok, who confronted Egypt's growing power on the river from the late 1830s to the end of the 1850s. At first Nyidhok held aloof from the merchants, confining them to the village of Kaka north of Pachodo or to river landings such as Kodok. He tried to enforce a royal monopoly on trade in ivory and firearms, with which he armed his own bodyguard, but this policy of restriction and containment failed. The royal monopolies prevented the emergence of a class of Shilluk merchants and encouraged Shilluk to join the traders for the goods they brought. Many were armed by the traders and joined their raids. Kaka increased in importance after the 1854 Egyptian ban on exporting slaves from Sudan, and the caravans between Hofrat en-Nahas in western Bahr el-Ghazal and Dongola on the Nile were rerouted through Kaka. Finally, after the death of Nyidhok in 1859 the Kaka merchants allied with dissident Shilluk and neighboring Baggara to seize control of the northern part of the kingdom (Mercer 1971, 419–26).

Both banks of the White Nile now came under Egyptian control, a shift in power marked by appropriating the royal name "Fashoda" for Kodok, the capital of the new province. The new reth, Kwathker Akwot, lived in semiexile in the south until he was captured and killed by the Egyptian governor. Throughout the rest of the nineteenth century the Shilluk kingdom was in a semi-perpetual state of civil war as government-appointed reths were never fully able to subdue rival claimants, many of whom conspired with the same government to depose or assassinate the incumbents (Pumphrey 1941, 4–5; Crazzolara 1951, 137).

The Shilluk experience was repeated with variations in many other parts of southern Sudan. In those parts of central and eastern Equatoria under the authority of rainmaker kings, the confrontation with merchant companies had a transformative impact on leadership.

Rain Kings, Cargo Chiefs, and Warlords

When the first Egyptian flotilla reached the Bari region of Gondokoro in 1841, the leading rain king was Logunu. He died soon afterward, and succession was contested by his two sons, Subek (also known as Jubek) and Nyiggilo, both of whom, in the local idiom, "had rain," though both also bolstered their claims and positions through alliances with the new companies coming to trade. Nyiggilo traveled to Khartoum, became useful to traders as an interpreter, and secured the passage of trade goods via his home in Bilinyan east to the Pari and Lotuho. The trading companies became increasingly involved in internecine wars between Bari chiefs, selling captives down the river to Khartoum. Despite their alliances with the trading companies, the careers of both Subek and Nyiggilo ended when their people accused them of failing to bring rain. Nyiggilo's murder in 1859 marked the eclipse of the power of the rain kings. Their place was taken by what Simonse has termed the "cargo chiefs," commoners drawn from a new class of Bari soldiers, interpreters, and auxiliaries in the orbit of the trading stations, whose power and influence were built on contacts with the trading companies and their ability to pass on "cargo": the cotton cloth, glass beads, copperware, and alcohol that dominated trade goods.[2]

Two of the most prominent cargo chiefs of the period from 1859 to 1883 were Loro-lo-Laku near the government station of Gondokoro and Laku-lo-Rundiyang at Rejaf. Both were commoners "without rain." Loro had been an interpreter for the traders, but he also had marriage connections with Nyiggilo's son, the rain king Bepo-lo-Nyiggilo at Bilinyan. Bepo used his collaboration with Loro to maintain trading with partners in the east. Some of these, the Lokoya and Lulubo in particular, adopted a deep rural strategy of avoiding direct contact with the trading companies while obtaining their goods indirectly from others.

A chief could provide some protection for his people from the depredations of government soldiers through his association with the government, but such association could also be personally dangerous. Loro was assassinated on the orders of the governor of Equatoria. His rival Laku sided with the government against the rebellion of Bari, Dinka, and Mahdist forces in 1884 but was killed by his own people, who switched sides and joined the government's enemies in 1885 (Simonse 1992, 99).

The collapse of the Egyptian administration and the end of the steamer-supplied cargo allowed the rain kings to regain some of their political power. Bepo led a multiethnic alliance in revolt against the government. But the alliance's political space was limited as a new group of warlord chiefs, the successors to the cargo chiefs, rose to power. The continued presence of contending militaries meant a ready supply of arms, ammunition, and recruits as soldiers moved back and forth between the Egyptian, Mahdist, and warlords' armies. This ready pool of multiethnic recruits enabled many warlords to bypass the age-set system in building their armed retinues. The career of the Bari warlord Mödi Adong Lado is illustrative of these "new men." Captured as a boy and taken to Khartoum, he was enrolled in the army and sent back to Equatoria. He was a useful interpreter for the Egyptian administration but switched sides and became a minor Mahdist commander. When the Mahdists were defeated at Bedden by the Belgians in 1897 he abandoned them and, taking his own army of fifteen hundred "ethnically diverse" soldiers, set himself up as an independent chief in alliance with a rain king (Simonse 1992, 103; Leonardi 2013a, 39).

The pattern of the Bari cargo and warlord chiefs was repeated in many other parts of southern Sudan as a new class of "trading chiefs" emerged (Leonardi 2013a, 32–39). In a sequence characteristic of politics in a tribal zone, the agents of the expanding state identified and elevated friendly collaborators, and these new men increased their status by securing a central position in trade relations as middlemen between the traders and their own people. New weapons and forms of warfare redirected support to the new leaders as old patterns of authority came under strain. Yet some of the older types of leaders also acquired weapons to bolster their authority, often in alliance with the new men.

The Zariba Network

The network of fortified commercial camps in the zariba system (Arabic plural *zara'ib*) defined the military-commercial character of slavery in nineteenth-century

Sudan. The system introduced southern Sudan to a network of international credit that connected the camps of the traders to commercial companies operating out of Khartoum, Egypt, and Europe—in effect the region's first banking system. It drew southern Sudan into an extractive international economy in which the territory's main exports were its own captured labor, ivory and other animal products such as ostrich feathers, rubber, iron, copper, and local food products such as tamarind (H. C. Jackson 1970, 8; James, Baumann, and Johnson 1996, 235): goods very similar to those that flowed in trade and tribute from Nubia to ancient Egypt.

It was through the zariba system that southern Sudan was conquered, pacified, and governed. It created contradictions in free and servile status. Free immigrants who were hired on as soldiers became bound by indebtedness to their employers, while slaves were armed by their captors and elevated to positions of power and authority. Indigenous cultivators and laborers lived in varying degrees of servitude depending on their proximity to the zara'ib. Many indigenous authorities lost their sovereignty as they were subordinated to the zara'ib, or were replaced by new men whose power lay in their willing collaboration with the zariba leaders and their ability to use that collaboration in commanding labor (Johnson 1992, 163).

Trading companies started moving out of the Bahr el-Jebel region as ivory supplies began to dwindle in the 1850s, and during the 1860s the companies expanded their network of fortified camps and caravan routes west and south through Bahr el-Ghazal into Dar Fartit and the Zande and Mangbettu kingdoms. The connection between ivory trading and slave raiding was established at the outset as companies forged alliances with local communities and joined them in raiding their neighbors. Cattle taken in these raids were used to feed troops, reward allies, and trade for ivory. Captives taken were given to company employees as slaves or sold (Gray 1961, 47–49). At first musket-armed northern Sudanese retainers formed the backbone of the companies' military force, but soon slave riflemen dominated the permanent garrisons of the zara'ib. In the 1870s the Egyptian administration took control of the camps and their armies until supplanted in the 1880s by invading Mahdist armies, who also based themselves in a few old zariba sites and absorbed the slave soldiers into their own *jihadiyya* (trained riflemen). It was the riflemen of the jihadiyya who gave the Mahdi's army the disciplined firepower to defeat Egypt's Sudan garrisons and enabled his successor, the Khalifa Abdullahi, to hold on to power (Johnson 1992, 165–70; Thomas 2010, 33).

The exemplar of the zariba system was Zubair Rahma Mansur, better known as Zubair Pasha. Arriving in Bahr el-Ghazal in 1856 as a member of an Egyptian merchant's expedition, he soon became a partner in the company before forming his own outfit. Establishing stations among the Golo and Kresh in Dar Fartit, by the mid-1860s he was in virtual control of much of

Bahr el-Ghazal. He secured access to the Zande trade by marrying the daughter of King Tikima. Zubair later quarreled with Tikima, killed him, and annexed his kingdom. His headquarters, Daim Zubair, was built on the strategic site of Gbaya where the north-south caravan route from Dar Fartit to Zandeland joined the east-west route to the Nile via Wau, Meshra el-Rek, Rumbek, and Shambe. When the government imposed stricter trade regulations along the Nile, he negotiated an alternative route with the Rizeigat Baggara through the southern Darfur province of Shakka, connecting with the Kordofan trade routes. It was along this route that Zubair invaded and conquered Darfur in 1873–74. When he was recalled and detained in Cairo by the Egyptian khedive, his trading empire incorporated much of Dar Fartit, the copper mines of Hofrat al-Nahas, a number of former Zande kingdoms, and territory both south and north of the Kiir/Bahr el-Arab, including the home areas of the Rizeigat and Humr Baggara, but not the Ngok Dinka (H. C. Jackson 1970, 4–68; Santandrea 1964, 24, 73–76, 285–86; Henderson 1939, 67–68).

The nineteenth-century trade networks resembled a spiderweb of caravan routes between the major trading posts, linking smaller subsidiary zara'ib. They created new networks that shifted regional connections and knitted different territories of southern Sudan together. Dar Fartit was detached from Darfur and incorporated into Bahr el-Ghazal. The Dinka of northern Bahr el-Ghazal came into contact with the Zande kingdoms along the

Nile-Congo watershed for the first time through their participation in trading caravans. The interior of Bahr el-Ghazal was connected to the Nile trading routes.

The zariba system created opportunities for new men and, on occasion, new women. Many of the agents in charge of the zara'ib either were drawn from the retinue of armed slaves or were subordinate indigenous leaders. Rafa'i Agha was one of the most successful of these agents. Variously described as a "negroid Muslim adventurer" and as the illegitimate son of a Sudanese trader, he commanded one of Zubair Pasha's western stations. Falling out with Zubair's son and successor Sulaiman, he allied with the Egyptian government in their campaign against Sulaiman in 1878–79. He was then sent back to Zandeland by the government to subdue the remaining independent kingdoms; he remained there until 1883, when he was sent to Rumbek to suppress the Agar Dinka rising and was killed (Evans-Pritchard 1971a, 335, 338, 344; Santandrea 1964, 33; Gray 1961, 158).

A son of a Zande king could also find preferment in the zariba system. Mbagahli Muduba was the younger brother of a Zande king allied to a trading company and learned Arabic while serving in the company's force of auxiliary spearmen. Given the Arabic name Surur and a mixed force of Nubian and Zande riflemen in 1870 he was put in charge of a deposed Zande chief's territory on the frontier with some of the most powerful Zande kingdoms (Schweinfurth 1874a, 450, 465–66, 470, 473; 1874b, 221–22; Gray 1961, 63).

Slave soldier agents were also used by the Egyptian government, but not all came from local communities. Bakhit Bey Batraki, the governor of one of the districts bordering Zandeland, was a Nuba veteran of the 1860s Mexican campaign and later died defending Khartoum from the Mahdists (Hill and Hogg 1995, 163–64). He built up a local following by distributing government largess, and it was later observed that Nuba and southern Sudanese officers in Egyptian service were able to associate more freely with the local communities they administered than Turkish, Egyptian, or Arab officials (Junker 1890, 356, 479–80).

Those outside the zariba system who benefited from it included Achol, a wealthy Dinka woman whose proximity to Meshra el-Rek (briefly renamed after her), extensive herds of cattle and flocks of sheep, and substantial holdings of copper and iron made her a welcome partner to the trading companies (Schweinfurth 1874a, 131–34). Further afield on the Bahr el-Zeraf, Nuaar Mer, a Dinka refugee adopted by the Gaawar Nuer, became the main intermediary with the companies briefly based there. Backed by the soldiers of the zariba, he held sway over the mixed Nuer-Dinka community of the Zeraf valley, amassed a large herd of cattle, and imitated his zariba allies to the extent of riding a horse (Johnson 1994, 128–30).

Close association with the zara'ib brought its own dangers. Achol was murdered by neighbors, who blamed her for bringing the "Turks" to their country (Schweinfurth 1874b, 338). The evacuation of the Bahr el-Zeraf zara'ib in the mid-1870s left their local allies weakened and targets of revenge. Deng Cier, a circumcised ex-soldier probably left behind from the Zeraf camps, was killed and his force scattered when he led a band of Dinka against the Lou Nuer prophet Ngundeng Bong (Johnson 1995, 212–14). Nuaar Mer was attacked and killed by a coalition of Nuer and Dinka led by the prophet Deng Laka, whose mother Nuaar Mer had sold into slavery (Johnson 1994, 133–37). In 1883 the Agar Dinka chief, Wol Athiaan, who had ambivalent relations with the commander of the Egyptian garrison at Rumbek, used his insider's knowledge of the zariba to lead another Nuer-Dinka coalition to assault and destroy the camp (Johnson 1993, 48).

The Zande Kings

The Zande kings, with their structured kingdoms and organized regiments, were initially in a better position both to benefit from and to contain the advancing trading companies, but their often fratricidal rivalries allowed the companies an entry point, leading to many of the kings' eventual subordination. The kings regarded the iron and copper they received in exchange for ivory as tribute, rather than trade. Ultimately, as the traders began taking hostages, enslaving captives, and plundering cultivations, the kings felt threatened and humiliated before their subjects (Evans-Pritchard 1971a, 310–11). Three of the most prominent Zande kings alternated between the strategies of resistance and accommodation.

Yambio Bazingbi, after whom the town of Yambio is named, and who is better known through his praise name of Gbudwe, was the archetypical resister. Gbudwe's father, Bazingbi, was at first friendly to the traders and, as so many other kings did, married one his daughters to a merchant. He was soon alienated by the behavior of the companies; he complained that "they summon me as though I were a dog," and instructed his son to attack them in 1866–67. Gbudwe inherited his father's kingdom and continued his war against not only the trading companies but also their Zande allies, defeating Mbagahli's brother, for instance, and annexing his kingdom (Evans-Pritchard 1971a, 290–93, 321–28).

Gbudwe's neighbor, Ndoruma Ezo, also initially held his own against the trading companies. Despite the merchants' efforts to prevent the Azande from getting firearms, Ndoruma managed to acquire some and used escaped Zande soldiers to train his own men. He relied on these riflemen in his successful wars against the companies in 1870–71, acquiring more rifles and attracting more fugitive slaves to his army, whom he trained and dressed like the soldiers of the zara'ib. In 1878–79 he sided with the Egyptian government in its war against Sulaiman Zubair (Schweinfurth 1874b, 298, 308–11, 497; Junker 1891, 101–3; Thuriaux-Hennebert 1964, 36, 270; Evans-Pritchard 1971a, 314, 317–18).

Tambura Liwa had direct experience of the power of the zariba armies when his father was killed by a rival who called on the aid of the trading companies during a succession dispute. Tambura was taken hostage and held captive in Daim Zubair until freed by Egyptian forces after the defeat of Sulaiman Zubair in 1879. With Egyptian support he retook his father's kingdom and that of his father's rival, reorganizing them into an administrative system adapted from Zubair Pasha (Evans-Pritchard 1971a, 271–72, 275; Santandrea 1964, 121–23; 1968, 42).

Both Ndoruma and Gbudwe felt the power of the new Egyptian regime in Bahr el-Ghazal when they were attacked by government troops led by Rafa'i Agha in 1881–82. At first they resisted together, but Ndoruma switched sides. Gbudwe ended up a captive and Ndoruma a subordinate chief to the government. Both kings regained their sovereignty with the fall of the government to the invading Mahdist army in 1885 and that army's recall to the Mahdist capital of Omdurman on the Mahdi's death. Released from captivity, Gbudwe returned to his kingdom and continued to expand it, holding it against other Zande kings and returning Mahdist invaders throughout the rest of the century. Both Ndoruma and Tambura, too, expanded their domains. Gbudwe remained a traditionalist and, unlike Ndoruma and Tambura, refused to arm his regiments with rifles (Evans-Pritchard 1962, 95; 1971a, 340–65; Santandrea 1964, 42; 1968, 42; Tucker 1931, 52–54).

The Nineteenth-Century Legacy

Displacement was the theme of the late nineteenth century. The activities of the trading companies, the new economic centers built by the zariba system, the campaigns of the Egyptian government, the intermittent interventions of the Mahdist state, and the opportunistic activities of the enhanced rulers and the new men left in their wake all contributed to a dispersal and recombination of populations. The slave trade and wars accounted for some of the depopulation reported by nineteenth-century observers, but it was also the result of whole populations moving away from zariba centers and caravan routes, becoming even deeper rurals, invisible in the forests, or seeking refuge with a succession of surviving potentates. What the zariba owners, new men, and Zande kings all had in common was basing political power on building "wealth-in-people" (Leonardi 2013a, 25). Thus the populations of Zande kingdoms became even more diverse, the old zariba sites would present the next generation of invaders with a puzzle of "tribal confusion" (Tucker 1931), and new communities of southern Sudanese diaspora were spread throughout the wider region.

5

Dispersal and Diasporas

War and slavery are two of the biggest factors in population dispersal and creation of diasporas, and in the Nile Valley war and slavery increasingly intersected during the nineteenth century with the proliferation of armies of slave soldiers. No one personified this better than the Shilluk officer in the Egyptian army who was among those who confronted Captain Jean-Baptiste Marchand's French force at Fashoda in 1898.

Born at the Shilluk royal capital of Pachodo in the 1830s, Lual Maiker first found employment with the Kaka merchants until he was captured by neighboring Baggara, paid as part of their tax to the Egyptian government, conscripted into the army, and given the name 'Ali Jaifun. "Soldiers ordered on service do not generally trouble their minds much about who their enemy is to be or why there is to be war, and we were no exception to the general rule," he later reminisced (Machell 1896, 184). Throughout the final four decades of the nineteenth century he found himself on garrison duty in Egypt or on campaigns throughout Sudan, in present-day Eritrea, and even in Mexico as part of the Egyptian battalion lent to the French, for which he was decorated by Emperor Napoleon III. By the end of his life he was the highest-ranking Sudanese officer in the Egyptian army. He died in the northern Sudanese town of Berber and was buried there (Hill and Hogg 1995, 164–65).

Slavery had long been a state institution of the Sudanic kingdoms. The formalized exchange of slaves for trade goods established by the Baqt treaty between Muslim Egypt and Christian Nubia in 652 CE set a pattern that would last for centuries, whereby peoples from a state's periphery were enslaved and passed through the state to other lands. As the slave-raiding frontier moved farther south with the establishment of the sultanates of Sinnar and Darfur, diaspora communities of enslaved peoples were created not only inside the Sudanic states but beyond the Nile Valley as well.

One of the first recorded diaspora communities was described by the Scottish explorer James Bruce when he encountered the semicircle of military encampments surrounding the Funj capital of Sinnar in the early 1770s. Referred to under the generic name of "Nuba," they were "purchased or taken by force" not only from the Nuba Mountains but from the southern Blue Nile foothills between Fazoqli and Jebel Moya. They lived unassimilated in their military villages, uncircumcised, speaking little Arabic, keeping herds of pigs, and following their own religions. Referred to by their overlords as both soldiers and unbelievers, their main role was to keep the sultanate's Muslim population "in subjection"

(Bruce 1790, 419–21, 425, 438, 443, 459). So dependent was the sultan on slave soldiers to maintain order in his realm that to this day there remains an ambiguity about who the Funj "really" were: Nubians from the north or black Africans from the south, and whether to be Funj meant to be free or slave (James 1977).

Histories of Population Dispersal

Slavery was only one cause of population displacement and amalgamation. The segmentary societies of the Dinka and Nuer were able to incorporate foreign individuals and whole foreign lineages. The ecologies of the eastern plains are such that any place that could support permanent settlement was occupied by a mixed population, and long-term survival depended on establishing links between groups pursuing different livelihood strategies in different ecological niches (Johnson 1989a). This involved the strategy of building "wealth-in-people," and, as Leonardi has explained, political power based on this strategy "*depended* on attracting non-agnatic followers" (Leonardi 2013a, 25). This is what the segmentary societies had in common with the Nilotic and Zande kingdoms, as well as the zariba owners and the new men who followed in their wake.

One of the most famous mass movements in nineteenth-century southern Sudan is the eastern migration of the Nuer, the subject of much ahistorical commentary in the secondary anthropological literature. At different times in the early nineteenth century, and for different reasons, various groups of Nuer crossed the Nile from their western homelands, forming new settlements in the east. A group of Jikany, having been defeated by their western Dinka neighbors, took advantage of a civil war in the Shilluk kingdom to move through Shilluk territory into the Sobat valley (Jal 1987; Stringham 2016). In midcentury other groups of Nuer, such as the Lou and Gaawar, similarly benefited from the disruption caused by the entry of the zariba system into the Sobat and Zaraf valleys to move into territories abandoned by their previous owners (Johnson 1982a; 1994, 44–55). The process of opportunistic settlement was not halted by the twentieth-century delimitation of a boundary between Sudan and Ethiopia. The combination of war and environmental change encouraged continued Nuer movement into Ethiopia from the twentieth into the twenty-first century (Johnson 1986b; Feyissa 2011; Falge 2016).

The Nuer migration was more a settlement than a conquest, and the indigenous Dinka and Anuak populations were as often rearranged as displaced. Assimilation into Nuer communities was achieved through adoption and intermarriage (Evans-Pritchard 1951, 19–20, 24–25), and in the long term the Nuer age-set system, in which young men were initiated with parallel marks cut into their foreheads, enabled foreign men to marry Nuer women and fight alongside their Nuer age-mates (Stringham 2016, chap. 3). As a result of assimilation and the creeping expansion of Nuer settlements, kinship ties cut across Nuer lineages and tribal boundaries. Some Nuer communities had closer links with near foreign neighbors than with more distant Nuer sections, thus increasing the likelihood of inter-Nuer feuds when Nuer sections defended their Dinka or Anuak kin against other Nuer raiders. By the beginning of the twentieth century, Nuer, Dinka, and Anuak communities lived interspersed and intermixed and Dinka was still widely spoken throughout the Nuer settlements. In the latter half of the nineteenth century, the Lou Nuer prophet Ngundeng attempted to formulate a philosophy of social harmony within this mixed population that not only condemned Nuer inter-sectional feuds but prohibited raids against non-Nuer neighbors. While ultimately unsuccessful in his lifetime, Ngundeng's teachings took on a new meaning and acquired a greater audience in the twentieth and twenty-first centuries as the Nuer became increasingly integrated into the wider South Sudanese society (Johnson 1994, chap. 3).

Zariba Populations

The slave trade was a more prominent feature in population dispersal in nineteenth-century Bahr el-Ghazal than in the eastern plains. Many communities fled to stronger neighbors for protection against the slave raids: some to the Zande kingdoms, others absorbed into Dinka lineages, still others grouped around the new men who acquired firearms and adopted the new methods of warfare. The Dinka chief Awutiek, known in the colonial literature as "Chak Chak," was the product of a mixed marriage, the son of a Jur mother. As the owner of a number of rifles, he offered protection to his neighbors in the slaving zone, receiving Ndogo and Woro Fartit refugees from the Mahdist incursion of 1885 and Ndogo, Golo, and Luo-Shatt during Tambura Liwa's Zande invasions in the 1890s (Comyn 1911, 150–51; Santandrea 1964, 54, 60, 206, 298). Kangi, a Jur war captain, gathered a following of Jur and Shilluk-Luo fleeing Dinka raids (Santandrea 1968, 73–74). Some Dinka even fled to the Jur, while Jur fled to the Bongo, and other Bongo fled to the Dinka (Schweinfurth 1874a, 238; 1874b, 270; Junker 1891, 77).

The greatest mixings occurred within and around the zara'ib themselves. Each station contained slaves captured from different communities and owned by the company employees, soldiers, and petty merchants (*jallaba*). Each station was further surrounded by concentric circles of subject peoples employed in providing food for the zariba inhabitants. The companies imported Dinka and even Rizeigat Baggara as cattle minders to look after their herds. Villages subdued by the companies were required to relocate around the stations, and as the zara'ib, too, frequently moved sites, their captive population moved with them. Rival companies often poached each other's subjects, and sometimes subject communities would decamp: changing masters, seeking protection from independent rulers, or fleeing into the forests (Johnson 1992, 167–70). So great was the population mixture that one traveler in 1880s Bahr el-Ghazal declared that accurate frontiers between tribes no longer existed (Junker 1891, 89).

The population mixing within zariba sites created a linguistic fusion, sometimes allowing for small acts of resistance. The Dinka ex-slave Salem Wilson recalled, "I learned a song from a Central African negro which had been specially composed against the slave-traders. . . . I used to sing this song to the men who had sold and bought me, and they never knew what it was about. I used to sing it with many quaint and grotesque gestures and grimaces, and they used to think it tremendously funny. So did I, and I got much satisfaction from singing it" (c.1939, 153–54).

The Proliferation of Slave Armies

In the nineteenth century the use of slave armies proliferated beyond the Nile countries into East and Central Africa. They contributed to the downfall of the indigenous states of Darfur, Bornu, and Bunyoro, and precipitated a dynastic change in Ethiopia. They were the powerbase on which new commercial empires rested, assisted both the rise and destruction of the Mahdist state, and were the coercive arm Britain and Germany used to establish their East African colonies. In each case the majority of soldiers in these armies initially came from southern Sudan (Johnson 1989b).

Egypt's creation of a permanent garrison in Sudan was the cause of the expansion of military slavery in Africa at a time when it was disappearing elsewhere in the Middle East. Egypt's Sudanese (or "Nubian") battalions were the model commercial companies adopted in building their own armies of slave riflemen in the south, and they also provided a reservoir of conscripts for other forces as soldiers moved between state, commercial, and independent armies.

The army of Zubair Pasha perhaps had the greatest impact on the history of the region. Originally composed of mainly Azande and Fartit, it also included a large number of Mandala. The Mandala formed one of the serf communities within the Darfur–Bahr el-Ghazal borderlands, runaway slaves who continued to pay tribute or owe services to their former Baggara masters. Zubair placed these men under the command of Rabih Fadl Allah, his most successful subordinate. Rabih was said to be of Hamaj parentage from the fringes of Sinnar, born in the undesirable "Salamat al-Basha" quarter of Khartoum—loosely translated as "the Pasha's How's Your Father" because of the number of brothels it contained (Hill 1967, 312–13). He joined Zubair in the 1860s and rose to prominence in battles in Bahr el-Ghazal and Darfur. He continued serving Zubair's son, Sulaiman, until the latter's defeat and execution by government forces. Gathering a contingent of Sulaiman's army and a number of Nubian merchants around him, he headed west on an exodus that would bring him to Bornu, which he conquered and ruled in the 1890s until defeated and killed by the French in 1900 (O'Fahey 1980, 89, 137; H. C. Jackson 1970, 24, 37–39, 47, 62; al-Hajj 1971, 132).

Two of Rabih's men who remained behind in Bahr el-Ghazal were Hamdan Abu 'Anja and al-Zaki Tamal, both Mandala clients of the Ta'aisha Baggara (Hill 1967, 147–48, 389). Having learned modern rifle warfare under Rabih they were an asset to both the Mahdi and his successor, the Ta'aishi Khalifa Abdallah, whose clients they were. Abu 'Anja was put in command of the Mahdi's jihadiyya, the trained riflemen taken on from private armies and captured government soldiers. Under his command they played a significant role in the defeat of Egypt during the Mahdi's rise. In the much disputed death of General Gordon it was most likely "a very tall black Sudanese" who fired the fatal shot that ended the siege of Khartoum and gave British imperialism a martyr to avenge (Johnson 1982b, 295). The Khalifa Abdallah's control of the jihadiyya through Abu 'Anja and al-Zaki Tamal was one of the main reasons he succeeded as head of the Mahdist state on the Mahdi's death in 1885 and was able to hold on to power despite domestic challenges. Abu 'Anja and al-Zaki Tamal led the invasion of Ethiopia in 1887–89, sacking the capital of Gondar, defeating and killing Emperor Yohannes IV at Gallabat, ending the Tigrayan dynasty, and opening the way for the Amhara ascendancy under Menelik II (Holt 1970, 63, 65, 73, 101, 135, 143–46, 153–55, 170–74).

Military Diasporas

The expansion in slave raiding, slave trading, and domestic slave owning in Sudan coincided with the rise of the international antislavery effort. Despite both Egyptian and Ottoman bans on the importation of slaves in the 1850s, Egypt's continuing need for slave soldiers to garrison its African empire meant that the extraction of slaves, mainly from southern Sudan, continued into the 1880s. Domestic slaves were also imported into Egypt and the Maghreb, the majority of them women. High mortality among slaves and low fertility among freed slaves meant that the slave and ex-slave population in nineteenth-century Egypt remained low (Baer 1967; Walz 1985).

By far the largest diaspora communities were those formed by the independent armies, who replenished and augmented their numbers through continuous slave raiding. When Rabih's army left Bahr el-Ghazal in 1879 it numbered some 800 to 1,000 men, drawn mainly from the Kresh and Dinka (Hallam 1977, 72). A decade later he claimed that his army was composed of "people of many races and various tribes," listing Banda, Kresh, and Ndogo along with undifferentiated Fartit (al-Hajj 1971, 138–39). Shortly before his final confrontation with the French it was reported that his army numbered some 5,000 gun men ("Shillooks, Dinkas, etc.") as well as 500 "Nyam Nyam [Azande] cannibals" (Anon. 1899).

Egypt contributed to these armies in various ways. Periodic financial retrenchment throughout the 1880s meant the downsizing of the Egyptian army but also created new revenue-raising opportunities through the renting out of demobilized Sudanese soldiers. Germany had an insufficient military force to confront the 1888–89 Bushiri rising along the Tanganyika coast and bought a recently disbanded Sudanese battalion from Egypt in order to suppress it. More Sudanese were recruited from Egypt to complete the conquest of Tanganyika and formed the core of the German African *Schutztruppe* (Wright 1993, 201–12). The Imperial British East African Company (IBEAC) also rented Sudanese soldiers from Egypt when advancing from Mombasa to Uganda. Financial considerations were among the reasons Egypt then allowed the transfer of its stranded Equatorial garrison to the service of the IBEAC, and these soldiers were subsequently formed into the Uganda Rifles (later the King's African Rifles) when Britain took over formal control of Uganda (Soghayroun 1981; Johnson 1989b, 2009a; Leopold 2005, chap. 6; 2007, 130–32).

In the colonial conquest of East Africa and the Anglo-Egyptian reconquest of Sudan, garrisons of southern Sudanese soldiers were instrumental not only in expanding the territory under imperial control but in securing the lines of communication that knit the conquered territories together. These garrisons became the nuclei of two distant but related communities of twentieth-century descendants of the nineteenth-century military slaves: the *malakiyyat* of Sudanese towns and the Nubis of East Africa (Johnson 2000a, 2009a).

The malakiyyat are products of Sudan's history of slavery and the army. They began as civilian, as distinct from military, settlements (Nakao 2013, 156), while among the Humr Baggara *melekiya* refers to the off-spring of freed slaves and is synonymous with *'abd,* slave (Cunnison 1966, 83). After the defeat of the Mahdist state in 1898, colonies of discharged soldiers were settled in malakiyyat around permanent garrisons and strategic stations in Omdurman, along the Blue and White Niles, and in Red Sea Province, where they acted as a reserve against local insurrections. In the south discharged soldiers and liberated slaves were settled in separate quarters within southern towns founded on the old zara'ib sites such as Taufikia, Kodok, Nasir, Mongalla, Rejaf, and Rumbek. The largest and most permanent quarters grew up in the main towns of Renk, Malakal, Wau, and Juba (Sikainga 2000; 2014, 63–65; Vezzadini 2015, chap. 9).

Sudanese settlements in Kenya and Uganda were located at first around the garrisons protecting the Uganda road from the coast or along the frontier with Bunyoro and Sudan. Up through World War I, discharged Sudanese were placed in special settlements, but in the 1920s and 1930s they were progressively confined to major towns: to Kibera on the outskirts of Nairobi, to Bombo and provincial towns such as Arua in Uganda.

The long-term survival of these communities derived from the fact that the slave armies were composed not only of soldiers but of the families and dependents of soldiers. Since the days of the zara'ib the civilian population of military stations outnumbered the armed residents. This civilian component included not only wives and children of the soldiers, but "followers": slaves and dependent widows and orphans. By the time the Equatorian garrisons moved into Uganda in the 1890s, their civilian "camp followers" outnumbered soldiers from 10:1 to 12:1 (Johnson 1992, 167–68). In Egypt and Sudan the transfer of Sudanese battalions between stations always involved transport for the *harimat,* the soldiers' wives and children. Throughout the reconquest of Sudan the soldiers acquired new wives and dependents after each victory, leading one observer to comment that "the path of victory is milestoned with expectant wives and children" (Steevens 1898, 14). Even the Sudanese soldiers recruited for service in Tanganyika brought their wives; a typical soldier's wife could be seen on campaign "carrying the child on her back, the sleeping mat, water container, cooking pot, and stirring spoon on her head" (Wright 1993, 186).

The women of these communities contributed to their distinctive character. Female slaves in nineteenth-century Cairo became known for their beer (*buza*) shops and their spirit possession (*zar*) performances (Walz 1985, 146), and the women of the zara'ib and the army harimat were also known for their entrepreneurial production of distilled alcohol and their organized spirit possession companies.

Women are the brewers of beer (*merissa*) in most southern Sudanese societies, just as they are in charge of most food preparation. Women ran the stills that produced araki and "Nubian Gin" (the precursor of

Uganda *waragi*) in the nineteenth-century zara'ib, the twentieth-century malakiyyat, and the East African townships (Schweinfurth 1874a, 238; Colchester 1950, 39). During the early part of the century the consumption of locally distilled spirits was closely associated with the military and the settlements of discharged soldiers (J. Willis 2002, 224). In Sudan it was particularly associated with the harimat of the Sudanese battalions. In 1930 one administrator in Malakal, the capital of Upper Nile Province, lamented "that a large number of women of the type of those of the [Omdurman-based] XIIth Sudanese [battalion] harimat live in Malakal, in fact there are quite a lot of that harimat and they were the people who resented interference with their araki-making so seriously as to pursue in a most dangerous manner the District Commissioner of Omdurman and the Police Officer" (C. Willis 1995, 319–20).

Colonial officials in Sudan recognized that the harimat were a force to be reckoned with and that most discontent within the Sudanese battalions stemmed from failures to provide adequately for them. Their ability to put pressure both on their husbands and on their husbands' superior officers was enhanced by the adoption of military hierarchies exercised by senior women, the *shaykhat*. An appeal to the shaykhat of the 11th Battalion's harimat is credited with ending the 1900 mutiny in Omdurman (Lamothe 2011, 78–89). The Tumbura spirit possession cults of the Sudanese soldiers and their descendants were and still are organized along military lines, supervised by shaykhat assisted by subordinates given military ranks (Makris 2000).

The social position of the internal diaspora in Sudan was ambiguous. In the early years of the Condominium they were the main support to the security forces and many rose to junior ranks in the army and administration. But their importance to the government declined as the Sudan garrison was gradually converted to locally recruited territorial units and finally detached from the Egyptian army in 1925, and as the sons of Sudanese soldiers more often took up nonmilitary work. With rural administration throughout Sudan increasingly organized around tribes, the urbanized "detribalized" diaspora had no clear place in the new structures of government, and were progressively isolated from their rural kin (Kurita 1992; 1997, chap. 2).

The East African Sudanese communities faced similar strictures but continued to grow and fashion a new identify for themselves. The terms Nubi and Sudanese are rooted in the history of slavery in Sudan and are derived from the Arabic terms "Nuba" and "Sudani" (black), both elastic terms applied at different times to slaves, the communities from which slaves were obtained, or communities of ex-slaves. In nineteenth-century Egypt, Sudanese army units were sometimes referred to as "Nubian," a blanket term applied to anyone from Sudan, not just Nubian speakers from the Sudan-Egyptian borderlands. But in the terminology of the southern zara'ib a distinction was made between the free Nubian soldiers enlisted from the north and the slave soldiers captured in the south. "Nubian," whether in English or Arabic (*Nubiyin*), thus had very different meanings depending on time and place.

"Nubi" and "Sudanese" were used interchangeably when describing the southern Sudanese diaspora in East Africa, but by the 1930s they increasingly insisted on calling themselves Sudanese. This was in part a response to the pressures placed on them by colonial governments. As the older army veterans passed away, and their sons sought other lines of work as traders, butchers, drivers, and mechanics, colonial authorities no longer saw the Sudanese as loyal servants but as unwanted immigrants. In Uganda government perceptions were guided by military needs, definitions of immigrant status, and the authority of the Buganda government in Native Administration (Hansen 1991). In Kenya these were related to land and the dangers of "detribalization" (Johnson 2009a).

The Sudanese in Kibera, originally bush land outside Nairobi, claimed that it had been given to them in lieu of a pension by the military authorities, a common practice at that time. As Nairobi began to engulf the township, the civil government viewed it as potentially prime real estate and wanted it back. In a contest that lasted decades and remained largely unresolved, the Sudanese referred to their past loyal military service under the British flag and asserted that they should not be treated as natives in the territories they had helped the

British to conquer. They claimed a national, rather than tribal, identity as Sudanese, and objected to being subject to labor dues in Buganda or native taxes in Kenya. It was only with the independence of these territories that the Sudanese diaspora began to reassert a tribal identity as Nubis, because their previous insistence on being considered a foreign nationality left them vulnerable to a loss of citizenship, especially in Kenya (Parsons 1997; Johnson 2009a; Balaton-Chrimes 2011).

In truth the Nubis could claim to be both foreign and native, because the Nubi communities in East Africa grew through the absorption of many indigenous peoples through the integration of slaves, military recruitment, and cultural assimilation (Meldon 1908). The anthropologist Mark Leopold characterized Nubi identity as "an elective, strategic, potential alternative ethnicity," and in northern Uganda "becoming Nubi" described the process of rural peoples moving to towns and adopting largely Nubi Muslim dress, customs, names, and language (2005, 15; 2007). The same phrase was used to describe southern Sudanese moving from the countryside to Juba in the 1960s, seeking protection from the ravages of the first civil war.

Language was an integrative factor in the malakiyyat and Nubi communities. Both "Juba Arabic" in South Sudan and Ki-Nubi in East Africa are evolving languages, derived from the military Arabic spoken by the southern Sudanese diasporas. A new language began to emerge within the zara'ib as early as the 1870s, influenced by the vernaculars of the captive communities (Marno 1873, 132; Leonardi 2013b). In common with most southern Sudanese languages, neither Juba Arabic nor Ki-Nubi use gender, and they have dropped verbal numbers, tense, and case, as well as distinctive Arabic consonants absent in vernacular languages (Meldon 1913; Nhial 1975; Mahmud 1983). "Juba Arabic" is in fact a misnomer, as there are dialectical differences between it and the Arabic spoken in Bahr el-Ghazal and Upper Nile. Ki-Nubi has also been strongly influenced by Swahili. The regional dialects of each language are similar enough to enable contact and intermarriage across borders (Manfredi and Petrollino 2013; Luffin 2013, 2014).

The Diaspora and the Failed Nationalism of the White Flag League

It was the diaspora's position between the emerging colonial elite and the urban artisanal class in northern Sudanese towns that placed it briefly in the forefront of Sudanese nationalist identity in the 1920s. During the long military confrontation between Egypt and the Mahdist state, when Sudanese battalions were permanently stationed on the frontier, a number of Sudanese soldiers rose to become officers in the Egyptian army. Sudan's immediate postconquest administration was essentially military, and sons of Sudanese soldiers were recruited into a new cadet corps and educated alongside sons of "the best families to be found in Sudan" to create a generation of modern state officials, the *effendia,* where the sons of slaves became colleagues of Egyptian officers and the sons of Arab notables (Kurita 1997; Vezzadini 2015).

The life of 'Ali 'Abd al-Latif has become emblematic of this new class and subject to a number of different interpretations. The most common is that 'Ali 'Abd al-Latif was a Dinka soldier whose loyalties were to the Sudanese nation as a whole. In reality his life was subject to a number of ambiguities.

'Ali 'Abd al-Latif's parents were slaves in Sudan's northern Dongola province. His father was from the Nuba Mountains, his mother a Dinka from Bahr el-Ghazal. They were swept up in the doomed Mahdist invasion of Egypt in 1889, where 'Ali's father was captured and conscripted into the Egyptian army and eventually obtained the rank of corporal. Like so many of his generation of Sudanese officers 'Ali was born in an Egyptian garrison and brought up in Egyptian garrison life until his father was demobilized and settled in a malakiyya colony.

It was through the patronage of one of his mother's cousins, a Dinka officer in the Egyptian army, that 'Ali obtained formal education in government schools and was commissioned as an officer in the army. He served in a variety of posts, both military and administrative, in Bahr el-Ghazal, the Nuba Mountains, Darfur, and the northern towns of Omdurman and Wad Medani. As an officer in a Sudanese battalion of the Egyptian army he owed his commission, and his loyalty, to the king of Egypt, not the king of Britain, and was a friend of Egyptian officers.

The officer corps in the Sudan garrison followed events in Egypt closely and was much affected by the postwar nationalism that eventually led to Egypt's qualified independence from Britain in 1922. This was followed by increased British investment in cotton production in Sudan in partnership with northern Sudanese notables, such as the leaders of the two main religious sects, Sayyid 'Abd al-Rahman al-Mahdi, leader of the Ansar, and Sayyid 'Ali al-Mirghanhi, leader of the Khatmiyya. It was also accompanied by political and diplomatic maneuvering to detach Sudan from Egypt (Johnson 1998b, xxxix–xli).

'Ali 'Abd al-Latif and a few colleagues in the effendia were influenced by these events and advocated "Sudan for the Sudanese," the term used for the first time to refer to all the peoples of the country rather than just the servile class of slaves and descendants of slaves. Following 'Ali's dismissal from the army for his political views he was a cofounder of the White Flag League, whose goal was a closer union with an independent Egypt. But the circumstances of the founding of the White Flag League illustrate the class and racial divide among the Sudanese effendia. When 'Ali 'Abd al-Latif objected that a fellow member of the Society of the Sudanese Union had addressed a volume of poetry to the "Noble Arab People" rather than the "Noble Sudanese People," the Sudanese

Union broke up, some going off with 'Ali to found the White Flag League, while other members of "good families" withdrew (Kurita 1989; 1997, chap. 1).

The question of "nobility" would be raised against the leaders of the White Flag League during the nationalist rising of 1924, when 'Ali, once again imprisoned, now became a popular rallying symbol for the urban working-class demonstrators of northern Sudanese and ex-slave origin. The rising was opposed by northern Sudan's leading notables who alluded to 'Ali 'Abd al-Latif's slave origins and dismissed the demonstrators as riff-raff. Their newspaper, *al-Hadarat al-Sudan* (The Civilization of Sudan), lamented, "Low is the nation if it can be led by 'Ali 'Abd al-Latif," and proclaimed that "the country is insulted when its smallest and humblest men, without status in its society, pretend to come forward and express the country's opinion" (Vezzadini 2015, 7). On 'Ali 'Abd al-Latif's release from prison he hoped to settle in the Nuba Mountains, where his father was born and where he owned land, but he was declared insane and exiled to Egypt, where he died in a mental hospital in 1948.

The early Sudanese nationalists failed to overcome the racial divisions bequeathed as a legacy of Sudan's history of slavery. 'Ali was described in one report as coming from the "dregs" of society, because of his servile origins, and rising to the "cream" through education and the army. While that personal trajectory made him a popular figure with some sections of society, questions of family origin, tribal belonging, and nobility of lineage prevailed. As a symbol of national unity he is an ambiguous one, as much a symbol of the country's fractures along regional, racial, and class lines as of its national aspirations. Yet no other political figure would symbolize the hopes of a united nation and be capable of drawing such enthusiastic crowds onto the streets of Khartoum until John Garang's arrival on 9 July 2005 to be sworn in as First Vice President in the government created by the Comprehensive Peace Agreement (CPA) at the end of the country's second civil war.

Banner of 'Ali 'Abd al-Latif and John Garang, Khartoum, 2005. *Photo by Douglas H. Johnson.*

6

The Dual Colonialism of the Condominium

The Anglo-French encounter at the river port of Fashoda in September 1898 was the most serious confrontation between major European powers in Africa before World War I, and parodied in W. C. Sellar and R. J. Yeatman's comic history of England, *1066 and All That* (1930), as "the only (memorable) *Incident* in History." To the Shilluk, and to their reth, Kur Nyidhok, it had a different significance.

Since midcentury no reth had been able to reign without the approval of the new external powers in the Nile Basin, whether the armies of the merchant companies, the Turco-Egyptian empire, or the Mahdist state. Nor was collaboration with these successive regimes a guarantee of survival. The Mahdists had installed and subsequently executed one reth before installing Kur in 1892 and giving him the Arabic name 'Abd al-Fadil. But the Mahdist garrison had just been expelled by Captain Marchand's Franco-Senegalese troops, who themselves were now confronted by an even larger force flying the Egyptian, not the British, flag. The officers commanding this Anglo-Egyptian contingent were British and Egyptian, but the majority of the soldiers were southern Sudanese. In fact, many were Shilluk, and their main intermediary was a Shilluk officer, adjutant major 'Ali Jaifun, veteran of many campaigns and the holder of two French medals, including the highly respected Médaille Militaire, whose career is briefly summarized in chapter 5 (Lamothe 2011, 180–83).

The fate of the French expedition would be decided within the chancelleries of Europe, but locally the garrison's survival depended on the Shilluk. While the British and French officers treated each other with the reciprocal courtesies of the European officer class, 'Ali Jaifun and the Shilluk soldiers apprised the reth and his people of the realities of the new power in the land. Reth Kur quickly assured them that he owed no allegiance to the French, and the local community boycotted the French garrison, selling their produce to the rival Sudanese camp, with whose soldiers they mixed freely (H. W. Jackson 1898, 97–98).

This opening encounter on the White Nile was symbolic of how southern Sudanese would experience the Anglo-Egyptian Condominium. Egypt, though still nominally part of the Ottoman Empire, was a British colony in all but name. The 1885 Congress of Berlin might have fired the starting gun for the European Scramble for Africa, but it was the collapse of Egypt's empire in northeast Africa that same year that opened up new territories worth scrambling for. By the 1890s not only did Belgium, France, and even Germany have ambitions to establish themselves along the headwaters of the Nile, but a resurgent Abyssinia laid claim to territory up to the White Nile. Britain countered these incursions by reasserting Egypt's old title to its abandoned empire.

Egypt's rivals for the headwaters of the Upper Nile were soon seen off: the French were forced to withdraw, the Belgians were restricted by treaty, and a boundary with Abyssinia was surveyed. With Egypt's interests in the south secured, Egypt's interests in the north domi-nated government policies throughout the rest of the Condominium period. Khartoum's policy for its south-ern provinces at first was exclusively concerned with security and obtaining the submission of indigenous peoples to imperial rule. Only halfway into the lifetime of the Condominium did government actively foster networks of formal native authority through which to govern, and only in its final decade was there a rapid acceleration in education, economic development, and administrative integration.

Pacification and Submission

With the 1899 Anglo-Egyptian treaty Britain grafted it-self onto Egypt's old empire. For the next half century southern Sudanese experienced the changing face of that empire, initially more Egyptian than Anglo, and more southern Sudanese than Egyptian. During the first two decades the peripatetic British inspector was only rarely seen. The main contact southern Sudanese had with government was through Egyptian and southern Sudanese subalterns: the mamurs (native officials), soldiers, police, and the Arabic-speaking ex-slave returnees from the north who became interpreters and chiefs (Leonardi 2013a, chap. 2). Local trade, when not conducted by northern Sudanese traders (jallaba), was in the hands of the commercial class of the old Ottoman Empire: Christian Greeks, Armenians, and Syrians.

The administration of the southern provinces for the first three decades of the Condominium was built on a pattern established in the nineteenth century. Old zariba sites were reoccupied and garrisoned. Light-skinned officers led units of dark-skinned riflemen on military patrols scarcely distinguishable from the raiding parties of the past, where, as one governor reported, "the inhabitants fled before the Government troops and returned to find their villages burnt and cattle vanished" (Johnson 1994, 10). As long as the role of the British inspector was that of "authorized cattle snatcher," one disgruntled official complained (Johnson 1994, 15), it was difficult for them to convince their new subjects that they were not the same as the old "Turks," whose flag they flew, whose soldiers they commanded, and whose resurrected claim to the territory of the upper Nile they now enforced. In many southern Sudanese languages the word "Turuk" came to mean—and still means—a light-skinned foreigner, a uniformed official, or an administrative bureaucrat, even when qualified by a phrase like the Nuer *Turuk col*, "black Turk."

The Shilluk soon had direct experience of what "submission" to the new authority meant. The British found three contenders for the Shilluk throne: all descendants of the long-lived Nyakwac. Suspicious of Reth Kur's dealings with both the Mahdists and the French they deposed him for alleged malpractices in 1903 and exiled him to Wadi Halfa on Sudan's Egyptian border, where he died in 1912. Choosing the brother of one of Kur's rivals to replace him, they restricted the succession to the kingship to descendants of the three contending families: a "tradition" that still applies. The new reth, Fadiat Kwathker, was the son of Nyidhok's successor. Though his powers were strictly limited within the new administrative structure, he reinforced his position through his friendship with the Egyptian soldier appointed as police officer in Kodok (the revived name of Fashoda river port), who learned to speak Shilluk long before any British official and married one of the reth's sisters.[1] When Reth Fadiet Kwathker died in 1917, the province governor intervened to ensure the election of a pliable candidate who promised to serve the government loyally (Stigand 1917).

Other kings fared less well. Shilluk military power along the White Nile had been broken in the mid-nineteenth century, but the Zande kings and princes along the Nile-Congo watershed still represented a formidable threat. The kings were just as divided against each other as they had been throughout the nineteenth century, but now they were also divided by their alliances with the different colonial powers. Ndoruma found himself on the Belgian side of the new international boundary. Tambura, an ally of the Egyptians before the Mahdiyya, found it easy first to ally with the French and then to submit to the new government after the French withdrew. Gbudwe was alone of the major kings to resist both the Belgian and the Anglo-Egyptian advances. He defeated a rival armed with Belgian rifles but failed to prevent the Belgian annexation of part of his kingdom. The final Anglo-Egyptian assault of 1905, assisted by Ndoruma's sons and Tambura's riflemen, ended in Gbudwe's capture and death (Evans-Pritchard 1957, 217–18; 1971a, 384–94). It was only in 1948 that his sons were permitted to construct a stone tomb over his gravesite in the town of Yambio, which now stands as one of South Sudan's few historical monuments.

The new government faced most resistance from those peoples, such as the Agar Dinka, who had resisted the old Turks and the Mahdists, or who, like the Murle, Anuak, and Nuer, had been barely touched by any previous government. Administrators frequently felt compelled to intervene in the intertribal disputes of transhumant cattle-keeping societies of Bahr el-Ghazal and Upper Nile provinces to support their tax-paying subjects against non-tax-paying opponents. Between 1899 and 1930 there were thirty-six military patrols and campaigns: against the Agar in 1902 and 1918; the Azande in 1903, 1904, and 1905; the Murle in 1908 and 1912; the Atuot in 1910 and 1917–18; the Anuak in 1912;

the Dinka of northern Bahr el-Ghazal in 1913 and 1922; the Lou and Gaawar Nuer in 1902, 1914, 1915, 1917, and 1927–30; the Lotuho, Lokoya, and Didinga in 1915–16; the Mandala of western Bahr el-Ghazal in 1918; the Aliab Dinka and the Eastern Jikany Nuer in 1919–20; the Twi Dinka of Kongor in 1921; and the western Nuer in 1923, 1925, and 1928. The very last "pacification" campaign in all of British Africa took place in southern Sudan, against the Nuer in 1928–30. In only eight of the first thirty-two years of the Condominium was there no significant armed confrontation between a southern Sudanese community and government forces.[2] In addition to these major campaigns there were the smaller patrols, armed marches, and police actions where tax was collected by force, unfriendly chiefs were deposed, and friendly chiefs were restored to office, or where "to restore order it was necessary to burn a few huts" (*SIR* 1921, no. 329, 4). It is no wonder that Evans-Pritchard reminded administrators a few years after pacification ended that "the Southern Sudan was conquered by force and is ruled by force, the threat of force, and the memory of force. Natives do not pay taxes nor make roads from a sense of moral obligation, but because they are afraid of retaliation" (1938, 76).

The Search for the Chief

Military administration persisted longer in southern Sudan than in the north. Even after the last soldier-governor retired in 1935, military officers continued to serve as district commissioners. But from a very early date the Condominium government advocated, if it did not fully practice, what the director of education in 1901 described as "the improvement of the native along the lines of his own institutions, and his own customs and regulations" (Johnson 2007, 312). Administration through native institutions meant first finding the leaders of those institutions.

British administrators throughout Sudan assumed that traditional tribal leadership had been disrupted by the Mahdiyya and set about trying to revive, with some modifications, what they thought had been the old order. Their experience with the Mahdiyya influenced them in other ways, in that they remained suspicious of and vigilant against any spiritually inspired leadership. In the south this meant that indigenous religious figures were often viewed as upstarts who had eclipsed the chiefs and distorted custom. Yet in attempting to resurrect a precolonial authority, officials often created new institutions of leadership.

Some of the first leaders to be recognized as chiefs by the government were the new men of the late nineteenth century whose authority rested on their possession of rifles or their knowledge of Arabic and ability to communicate with officers of the new administration. Most of the early Bari chiefs recognized by government were men like Mödi Adong Lado who did not "have rain" but held power as warlords, or were descendants of cargo chiefs (Simonse 1992, 103; Leonardi 2013a, 39). In the neighboring West Nile district of Uganda, Nubi agents were among the first government-appointed chiefs (Leopold 2007, 132–34). Not only was the Jur war captain Kangi in Bahr el-Ghazal recognized as a chief in his lifetime, but his descendants established a new chiefly lineage (Santandrea 1968, 73–74). In Upper Nile a former Egyptian army quartermaster-sergeant, Faragalla Buluk Amin (Nuer name Cany Reth) was made a chief among the Gaawar Nuer because of his literacy in Arabic (Coriat 1993, 19–20), while a former crewman on Egyptian and Mahdist riverboats, Mabur Ajuot, was an early government ally and chief of the neighboring Dinka (C. Willis 1995, 425). Even after rural administration became based on customary law administered through customary courts, one Gaajak Nuer veteran of the Turco-Egyptian, Mahdist, and Anglo-Egyptian armies, Faragalla Kong Dungdit, was retained as a chief over a section of Lou Nuer (C. Willis 1995, 419–29).

In the 1920s Native Administration became the policy throughout Sudan, applied in both the northern and southern provinces. Hierarchies of indigenous leaders were organized into local courts hearing cases according to local custom, supervised by district commissioners who, in addition to having to learn Arabic, were now also required to learn the vernacular language of their district where a separate vernacular existed. Egyptian mamurs were withdrawn along with the Egyptian battalions in 1925, the role of Sudanese mamurs was reduced, the old Sudanese battalions were disbanded, and security in southern Sudan devolved to the locally recruited Equatorial Corps and police under British officers (Daly 1986, 360–79).

It is often claimed that southern Sudan was administered separately from the north. This was not the case. Administrators were recruited from the same manpower pool of the army and university graduates and were subject to the same administrative regulations. Governors and deputy governors of southern provinces all had experience in northern provinces. What made the northern provinces distinct from those in the south was Arabic as a widely understood lingua franca, and the application of colonial versions of Islamic law alongside local custom, both of which facilitated the rotation of administrators between provinces. In southern provinces many district officers remained in the same province throughout their careers because of their knowledge of southern vernaculars. Few senior administrators in the secretariats in Khartoum had direct experience of the south, making the direction of central government policy more oriented toward northern than toward southern concerns.

In the southern provinces administrators frequently complained that, except for the Shilluk and Azande, most southern peoples lacked an executive figure who could collect taxes, organize *corvée* labor, or enforce government orders. Even the Shilluk and Zande kings had had their independent powers restricted, and among Nuer and Dinka pastoralists the men with the greatest

108

authority were prophets such as Guek Ngundeng and Dual Diu among the Nuer and Arianhdit among the Dinka. These latter suffered from the structural hostility of the government against ecstatic religious figures and were either killed or arrested and exiled in a series of military patrols throughout the 1920s (Johnson 1981, 514–17; 1994, chaps. 4–6; Mawut 1983, chap. 4).

The Southern Policy

The Southern Policy announced by the civil secretary in Khartoum in 1930 followed the logic of Native Administration in its stated intent to build up "self contained racial or tribal units" based on "indigenous customs, traditional usage and beliefs."[3] Giving priority to indigenous customs and beliefs included restricting the spread of the Arabic language and the Muslim religion by reducing the number of Sudanese administrative staff and controlling the number of northern merchants in the southern provinces, encouraging the use of both English and vernacular languages in administration and education, and adopting customary law in the customary courts. The policy has often been measured more by its intent than by its outcome. In force for only sixteen years, it had mixed results, never completely isolating southern Sudanese communities, excluding Muslim Sudanese, or preventing the use of Arabic.

There were immediate problems in building up self-contained tribal units. Not only had many populations become mixed during the events of the nineteenth century, but pastoralist societies were in periodic movement and impossible to isolate. Extreme attempts to separate peoples by imposing a "No Man's Land" between them failed. In the early 1930s Dinka communities living among the Nuer in Upper Nile Province were forcibly relocated south of an artificial No Man's Land separating them from the Gaawar and Lou Nuer. Within a few years they had returned to their original homes, the No Man's Land was abandoned, and province administrators encouraged further amalgamation of Nuer and Dinka societies (Johnson 1982a). At the same time the governor of Bahr el-Ghazal created a cultural and religious No Man's Land between western Bahr el-Ghazal and Darfur (often cited as typical of Southern Policy), separating groups of Fartit by forcing Muslim communities to go north into Darfur and non-Muslims to relocate along the roads to the south. This boundary was nevertheless porous and required continuous monitoring and readjustment as peoples in the north sought access to resources in the south (Sikainga 1983; Thomas 2010).

The difficulties affecting the Bahr el-Ghazal–Darfur border were repeated in other futile attempts to create hermetically sealed southern provinces composed of self-contained racial or tribal units. The Seleim Baggara were originally included in Upper Nile Province, were then incorporated into neighboring White Nile Province, but continued to use dry season pastures in Upper Nile and, to a lesser extent, intermarry with the

110

Shilluk and Dinka, a fact that many later used in their attempt to claim the right to vote in the 2011 southern independence referendum. The Upper Nile administration had ambitions to include the Mabaan, Uduk, Koma, and Ingessana of Blue Nile province, and for a time all these peoples were regarded as "belonging to the Southern Sudan" even while being administered by a northern province. Eventually the Mabaan, Uduk, and Koma were transferred to the Upper Nile administration, only for the Uduk and Koma to be returned to Blue Nile in 1953, shortly before Sudan's independence (C. Willis 1995, 345; James 1988, 257–58; 2007, 21–23). In 1913 the Nuba Mountains were detached from Kordofan and administered as a southern province until being reabsorbed into Kordofan in 1928. The Ngok, Twij, and Rueng Dinka were included in Kordofan in 1905 but over the next twenty years were reassigned to Bahr el-Ghazal, Nuba Mountains, Kordofan, and Upper Nile provinces until only the Ngok remained in Kordofan (Johnson 2010, 2012). In 1918 the Malual Dinka grazing land south of the Kiir/Bahr el-Arab was annexed to the Rizeigat of Darfur, a seizure that remains contested today and required numerous grazing agreement readjustments as both peoples continued to use the disputed territory (Kibreab 2002, 80–100; Johnson 2009b; Vaughan 2013).

It was never possible to exclude transhumant Arab Muslim pastoralists from entering the southern provinces. The number of northern Sudanese junior administrators working in the south was reduced, but not eliminated altogether. Ibrahim Bedri, who later founded the proindependence Socialist Republican Party in the 1950s, served as a mamur in various Dinka districts in the 1930s and 1940s, spoke Dinka, published articles on Dinka religion and history (Bedri 1938; 1948), and trained southern administrators, including Clement Mboro, later a leading politician and minister of the interior. Most of the technical staff in the Sudan Railways and Steamers, Posts and Telegraphs, Public Works, Egyptian Irrigation, Medical, and other departments came from northern Sudan.

There is as yet no thorough study of how permits of trade were issued during the Condominium, how many and what type of merchants were issued permits, but province and district records indicate that mainly well-capitalized Khartoum and Omdurman companies were issued trade licenses, whether owned by Greeks, Armenians, Syrians, or northern Sudanese. Many of the traders who operated in the smaller towns and rural areas were in fact Muslim southern Sudanese agents of the larger houses, recruited from the malakiyyat. Some even set up in business on their own, such as Rahmatalla Surur, a Muslim Shilluk who was based in Akobo for over forty years, became the chief merchant in town, was fluent in Anuak, Murle, and Nuer, and employed a Muslim Anuak as his agent in Pibor (Tunnicliffe 1933; Grover 1946; Lyth 1954).

Administration under Southern Policy generally had a more positive impact in the field of customary law. Because customary law differed not only between major language groups, but even between tribes speaking the same language, this was an area where government-appointed chiefs had the greatest influence, and where they were most effective in standing between their people and the forces of government. District administrators were required to function in the vernacular, though not all were fully fluent (Deng and Daly 1989, 170) and relied on the chiefs for details of precedents and interpretations of custom. Recording customary law was a continuous process and only began to show tangible results toward the end of the Condominium (Howell 1954; Johnson 1986a). The preservation of customary law is, however, remembered as one of the more benign legacies of British administration. Many Nuer make a distinction between "the government of the left," the positive peacekeeping network of chiefs, courts, police, and district officers, and "the government of the right," the coercive force of the army (Hutchinson 1995, 110).

Educational policy in the southern provinces had more ambivalent results. As early as 1904 the governor-general of Sudan declared that there was a need for only some "moderately educated Blacks" to fill minor official posts in the south (Sanderson and Sanderson 1981, 59). The government invested very little directly in education in the southern provinces, subcontracting it to missionary societies. Unlike the educational policy in the northern provinces the overall policy for the south focused on vernacular education as a barrier to "de-tribalization." As the secretary of education explained during the first years of the Southern Policy, "Our education must be directed to making the individual first of all a good tribesman—a good villager; to send him back contented to his tribe to live an improved life in his normal environment" (Winter 1933).

Such a restrictive approach did not allow for students to graduate to higher levels of schooling. Only a small number attended the church-run intermediate schools where instruction was in English and where the first cadre of southern teachers, clerical staff, and junior administrators were trained.[4]

Not all administrators agreed with the limitations of Southern Policy. The emphasis on vernacular education was already being reversed by the late 1930s, and the need for a more progressive educational policy in the south was recognized in Khartoum even before the end of World War II. Throughout the early 1940s administrators in the South were becoming more vocally critical of the lack of development policies for their provinces (Collins 1983, chap. 7). Pressure from within administration weakened Southern Policy's rationale, but its final demise was brought about by the postwar challenges of Egyptian and northern Sudanese nationalism. Egypt's attempt to reassert its sovereignty over the whole of Sudan forced British administrators into an uneasy alliance with the anti-Egyptian faction of northern Sudanese nationalists. The ramifications of Anglo-Egyptian rivalry for the support of Sudanese political factions would bring southern Sudanese into the center of Sudanese political life from which they had been excluded.

The Politics of Competing Nationalisms

The 1947 Juba Conference was deadlocked. It was the first time members of the northern and southern Sudanese educated elites had formally met together to discuss the future of their country. The British administration had already decided to hand power over to the northern Sudanese elite in order to prevent Egypt from gaining control of Sudan but only at this point decided to gauge educated southern opinion. The southern delegates to the conference expressed strong reservations about their future in a self-governing Sudan and about taking part in an appointed legislative assembly where they feared they would be outmaneuvered by the better-educated and more experienced northern politicians. Stanislaus Paysama, who would later become a senator and a leading figure in South Sudan's first political party, was then an administrative assistant in the civil secretary's office in Khartoum. He was instructed to make travel arrangements for the delegates to return to their homes, as no further progress seemed likely. He went to see the leading Umma Party delegate, Judge

Muhammad Shingeiti. Shingeiti "got up very angry and threw a piece of paper," he later recalled, "and said, 'Look, ya Stanislaus, your people are so dull, so stupid that they cannot understand how things are getting on. Why should not the Southerners join the Assembly together with their Northern friends? They will sit down there like anybody else, and they will put forward their case. The Northerners should listen to it. We are all Sudanese'" (Dellagiacoma 1990, 52).

Paysama then met with the southern delegates along with some hundred junior officials who debated what to do until early in the morning.

> At last Chier [*sic*] Rihan the Dinka chief, who was the oldest in the conference, got up and said: "Gentlemen, we now have stayed too long. Why should we be afraid of the Northerners? What I know is that . . . if the Northerners want to make injustice to us, well, we have young children, young men: they will take up the response and fight them; they are men like ourselves."
> So Deng Tong concluded: "Let us go to Khartoum and, if necessary, we shall organize the fight to defend ourselves. And let us end with this conference." (Dellagiacoma 1990, 53)

Stanislaus Paysama's eyewitness account of these backroom meetings during the Juba Conference, recorded shortly before his death in 1987, is important for two reasons. First, it has long been assumed that

Judge Shingeiti had lobbied the southern delegates that night and won them over with the promise of higher salaries (Robertson 1974, 108), but the southerners made their decision on quite different grounds. Second, Shingeiti's promise of a fair hearing in the legislative assembly would ultimately be proven false, while Cier Rihan's words would turn out to be prophetic.

Anglo-Egyptian Competition

The claims of Egyptian and Sudanese nationalism dominated nationalist politics from the 1920s through the 1940s. In treaty negotiations each of the condominium partners asserted its own right to represent the interests of the Sudanese, and this competition was reflected in the factional contests of Sudanese nationalists as they aligned themselves either with Egypt or with Britain to gain an advantage in their internal political struggles (H. Ibrahim 1976; Abu Hasabu 1985; Jal 1989; Kurita 1989). Southern Sudanese added a third, often ignored, voice to the debates only after the principle of Sudanese self-determination had been recognized.

Egyptian and Sudanese nationalist understandings of self-determination were influenced by international debates. The 1918 Soviet constitution recognized self-determination as a national "right"; the Treaty of Versailles espoused it as a "principle"; and it gained a precise definition in the Anglo-American Atlantic Charter of World War II, which affirmed the right of nations to self-government and self-determination within their geographical boundaries. The objective of that document was to free European nations then under German occupation, but it had immediate ramifications within Britain's own empire. Northern Sudanese activists were among the first of Africa's nationalists to apply the Atlantic Charter to themselves and request national self-determination. Their petition was rejected by the wartime Condominium government, but their actions placed self-government and self-determination on the postwar agenda (Woodward 1979, 23–27; Johnson 1998b, xlv–lii, 1–33, documents 1–13).

When Egypt tried to reassert its sovereignty over Sudan in 1946, Britain reversed its position and conceded Sudan's right to both self-government and self-determination. Sudan was offered the choice of union with Egypt or independence (Woodward 1979, chaps. 2–3; Johnson 1998b, lii–lx, 131–35, 137, 141–42, documents 1–3, 51–52, 54, 58)—prefiguring the choice offered South Sudan in the 2011 referendum, of unity within Sudan or independence.

But which Sudanese would exercise these rights? Both Egypt and the nationalists were united in insisting that Sudan should exercise self-determination within its geographical boundaries. Ismail al-Azhari, leader of the pro-Egyptian faction of nationalists, had declared "above all, the economic need of the North for the South" (Johnson 1998b, 57, document 26). In an interview with the British minister responsible for negotiating with Egypt, Sayyid 'Abd al-Rahman al-Mahdi, the posthumous son of the nineteenth-century Mahdi and the patron of the anti-Egyptian Umma Party, and Judge Shingeiti, a former member of the Society for Sudanese Union who later played a prominent part in the Juba Conference, had been more revealing of northern Sudanese attitudes toward southern Sudanese than they perhaps intended. Shingeiti boasted of Sudan's Arab ancestry and "spoke very contemptuously of Abdel Latif (now in an insane asylum). He said his mother was a negress, his father was unknown, and that he, Latif, had at one time collected old tins from barracks." When the discussion touched on southern Sudan, Sayyid 'Abd al-Rahman "indicated that they, the North, could deal with it very satisfactorily. The people in the south were called slaves," though Shingeiti, who was interpreting, hastily added that the term was scarcely used now (Johnson 1998b, 235–36, document 116).

Educated South Sudanese had been excluded from discussions within the advisory councils that led to decisions about self-government and self-determination (Collins 1983, 273–76). The 1947 Juba consultative conference involved senior British administrators, select northern Sudanese, and southern junior officials and chiefs, but the agenda left very little to discuss: the Southern Policy of restricted development in the southern provinces had been repealed, and self-government was going to take place with or without southern participation. In the end, after expressing strong reservations, as Stanislaus Paysama recalled above, the southern delegates agreed to take part in the legislative assembly being established in Khartoum in order to safeguard their interests.

The Emergence of South Sudanese Political Consciousness

In his stimulating study of class and power in Condominium Sudan, Tim Niblock asserts that South Sudanese political organization "evolved not as part of the Sudanese nationalist movement, but in reaction to it" (Niblock 1987, 157). It is more true to say that in the pre- and immediate postindependence period South Sudanese politicians attempted to redefine Sudanese nationalism in order to find a place within it.

Nineteenth-century South Sudan had been partially knit together by a tenuous commercial network, stronger in the west than in the east, where it was largely nonexistent. The Egyptian empire grafted itself onto that network shortly before the Mahdiyya in the north precipitated the rapid collapse of that empire. The Mahdist state never fully replaced the Egyptian garrisons it expelled from the south, occupying only a few outposts that it used as raiding centers. During the Reconquest of Sudan Britain quickly reestablished Egyptian authority in the north, east, and west but took far longer to assert control over the south. The memory of a long period free from external rule, more than the short-term effects of the brief period of restricted development under the Southern Policy (1930–46) was why South Sudanese felt they were not fully part of a Sudanese state when post-war nationalism began to wash over them, insisting that they were "all Sudanese." It is also why after attempts at inclusion failed South Sudanese leaders would later frame their own argument for self-determination in the post-war language of anticolonialism and anti-imperialism.

Those at the forefront of South Sudanese political consciousness were a new generation, most of whom were the early products of mission education. Only some, such as Cier Rehan (Dinka), James Tambura (Azande), Andrea Gore (Bari), or Edward Odhok (Shilluk), came from chiefly families, as it was not until the late 1940s that chiefs were pressed by the government to educate their sons. A few came to education in roundabout ways. Stanislaus Paysama was a Fur ex-slave, freed by the government in Bahr el-Ghazal and raised and educated by the Catholic mission. Buth Diu (Nuer) had been a district commissioner's servant and was educated by that official's wife. Most came from schools located among the permanent settlements of agricultural peoples in Bahr el-Ghazal and Equatoria, and either were employed by the churches that had educated them (both Paulo Logali and Benjamin Lwoki worked in Church Missionary Society institutions) or, like Clement Mboro, became junior civil servants.

The first active South Sudanese organization was the South Sudan Workers Association (SSWA) formed in 1946 by Stanislaus Paysama, Clement Mboro, Paulo Logali, Buth Diu, and others to represent the interests of southern government employees (Garretson 1986, 182–83; Arop 2012, 26). Some members of the SSWA took part in the 1947 Juba Conference and along with others were elected by their province councils to serve in the legislative assembly in Khartoum. Outside the assembly, political committees were formed in Juba and other main towns—the first South Sudanese political organizations. The committees forwarded petitions on a variety of political issues to the governments in Khartoum, London, and Cairo.

Southern members in the legislative assembly were outvoted by their northern colleagues on the creation of a Ministry for Southern Affairs and on drafting a federal constitution. The northern parties then outmaneuvered them in 1953 by signing a separate "All Parties Agreement" with Egypt that removed provisions from the Self-Government Statute that South Sudanese believed were essential for safeguarding their interests in the period leading up to self-determination. It was after being excluded from these negotiations that the political committees merged into the Liberal Party to contest the 1953 elections. Its leadership was exclusively South Sudanese, but its choice of name was intended to attract members from other parts of the country. Chronic funding problems and interprovincial leadership rivalry undermined political unity, and there were regular defections by South Sudanese parliamentarians to the government parties both before and after independence in 1956 (Bob and Wassara 1989, 297–304).

Sudan's Missed Opportunity

The parliamentary period of the 1950s was a window of opportunity in which Sudan's political leaders might have fashioned a system of government that could have preserved national unity. It was an opportunity they comprehensively missed.

The formation of the first all-Sudanese cabinet under the pro-Egyptian National Union Party (NUP) of Ismail al-Azhari in 1954 hastened South Sudanese political thinking toward federation and self-determination. Southerners initially advocated delaying self-determination, deploying the same developmental arguments voiced at the 1947 Juba Conference—that the South was neither economically nor administratively ready to participate on an *equal* basis with the North in an independent Sudan. With self-government a fait accompli, federation now emerged as the *condition* for South Sudanese participation in self-determination for Sudan as one country. Failing that, the only acceptable alternative to federation was a separate self-determination for the South (Johnson 2014, 9).

In their consistent opposition to any concession to South Sudanese demands, northern leaders unwittingly reinforced separatist ideas. The legislative assembly banned the use of the noun "South" in official documents, replacing it with "southern provinces," and in Sudan's first parliament the NUP leader of the House of Representatives criticized southern representatives for using the words "South" and "Southerners." "These words," he proclaimed, "could not come from a person who believed in the unity of the country. It was far better that they should say that they wanted a country of their own" (Parliament of the Sudan 1954, 222).

South Sudan's preferred options were clearly articulated in the first ever pan-South Sudanese conference held in Juba in October 1954. Liberal Party leaders organized the conference for South Sudanese of all parties and of none, of chiefs from the rural areas, and of the diaspora in the northern towns to decide a common position on the issue of Sudanese self-determination: whether to opt for union with Egypt or independence. The conference was a watershed in the history of South Sudanese political discourse. Political positions were articulated that resurfaced in political debates over the next fifty years. The conference overwhelmingly reaffirmed support for an independent Sudan under a federal system that would cover South Sudanese as well as the Nuba, Fur, and peoples of the Blue Nile. If federation was not granted then separation was the only alternative.[1]

Parliament approved a self-determination motion in August 1955, just as news of the outbreak of a mutiny of southern soldiers in Torit and disturbances in other parts of the South reached Khartoum. The 1955 disturbances posed a political challenge to the condominium partners, the government in Khartoum, and the northern and southern parties. The mutiny quickly collapsed but its impact accelerated the withdrawal of the condominium powers and circumvented the complicated self-determination process for Sudan agreed on in 1953.

The NUP had already abandoned its pro-union policy, and a clear majority of members of parliament favored independence. The two houses of parliament exceeded their mandate when they voted for independence on 19 and 22 December with major constitutional issues still unresolved. Southern parliamentarians threatened to vote against independence but voted in favor after receiving a weak assurance that the federal system would be "given full consideration" by a future constituent assembly (Johnson 1998c, 493–94, document 432, 497–501, documents 435–37). Sudan became independent thirteen days later on 1 January 1956.

South Sudanese focused on raising unresolved constitutional issues during the brief postindependence parliamentary period (Rolandsen 2010, 2011a). They advanced federalism as the preferred option of the 1954 Juba Conference, and argued their case emphasizing differences of race, language, culture, and religion (Mayom 1957)—categories the UN would later recognize as qualifying a people for self-determination. Northern Sudanese almost universally equated federation with separatism (Beshir 1968, chap. 11), and even moderate federal demands were treated as subversive. Parliament rejected the federal option in 1957.

South Sudanese now organized a more focused political effort and returned a large pro-federal bloc to the constituent assembly in 1958. The old generation of South Sudanese political leaders who had first articulated South Sudanese aspirations but who had been outmaneuvered in parliament were being displaced by a new generation of more militant, better-educated leaders like Fr. Saturnino Lohure, Joseph Oduho, and Ezboni Mondiri, all of whom would later take the lead in the exile politics of the 1960s.

In parliament South Sudanese reached out to other non-Arab regional parties such as the Nuba in Kordofan and the Beja Congress in eastern Sudan. The political leaders in these regions also felt alienated from the idealized Arab nationalism of the mainstream parties and excluded from the center of power in Khartoum. The pro-federal bloc in parliament was strong enough to prevent the passage of a unitary constitution, precipitating an army coup under General Ibrahim Abboud in 1958 (Bob and Wassara 1989, 304–7).

The political significance of the period between the end of the 1955 disturbances and the beginning of the first civil war in the early 1960s has often been underappreciated (Rolandsen 2011a). The military government disbanded parliament and denied the public a legitimate forum for discussion of any political options for maintaining the unity of the country other than through military force. The window of opportunity was firmly shut. It made the creation of a South Sudanese armed opposition inevitable.

Politics of the First Civil War

The southern provinces were not the only underdeveloped regions of Sudan, but they were among the least integrated into the national economy. The decision in the mid-1940s to use funds generated from the northern economy for accelerated economic and educational development in the South had put an end to any realistic prospect of separating the southern provinces from Sudan (Collins 1983, 276–77), but the design of the projects did little to promote economic integration. The original intention of the Zande Scheme in western Equatoria had been to provide the South with locally manufactured rather than imported goods (Reining 1966). The proposed Jonglei Canal was intended to benefit the agriculture of the northern provinces and Egypt, not the South (El Sammani 1984; Lako 1985; Howell, Lock, and Cobb 1988; Collins 1990). Modest programs with a local impact, such as the Yirol Co-operative Marketing Society (SDIT 1955, 131), received far less support. The new national government offered no alternative to the colonial-era projects, and the lack of any coherent development policy contributed to South Sudanese political grievances.

With no public forum for debate, South Sudanese politicians either went into exile or operated underground. The Sudan African National Union (SANU), formed in exile by Joseph Oduho, William Deng Nhial, and Aggrey Jaden in 1962 as the political wing of the armed opposition, publicly advocated independence for the South. A new generation of southern professionals and civil servants based mainly in the North created a network of political cells that kept in contact with the exile leaders. When Abboud's military regime fell in 1964, the network of cells emerged as the Southern Front with a cadre of leaders drawn from around the South, including veterans such as Clement Mboro, Ezboni Mondiri, and Gordon Muortat Mayen, and younger professionals such as Darius Bashir, Abel Alier, Bona Malual, and Hilary Paul Logali.

An attempt was made to reach a political solution for the "Southern Problem" at the 1965 Round Table Conference of the internal and exile parties in Khartoum. The conference got no further than each party stating its position, and no compromise was reached. The Southern Front and William Deng both advocated federalism, which was rejected by the northern parties. SANU split; William Deng stayed inside the country to contest elections while Jaden and Oduho remained in exile.

The Southern Front and SANU-Inside were closer in their positions than were the two factions of SANU but remained electoral rivals. SANU's support was concentrated mainly in Bahr el-Ghazal and Upper Nile. The Southern Front won fewer seats but drew its support more evenly from across all three southern provinces. SANU's willingness to collaborate with the northern opposition ended with William Deng's assassination by the army shortly after the 1968 elections. The two parties formed a combined delegation under Abel Alier in the constitution draft committee of the assembly, and walked out together when the assembly passed a draft Islamic constitution. The draft constitution and growing political protest in the east, the Nuba Mountains, and Darfur precipitated another military coup, bringing Ja'afar Nimeiri to power in May 1969 (Alier 1990, 40–42).

The Addis Ababa Agreement

Nimeiri's May Revolution promised a political solution to the civil war that had been fought in the southern provinces for nearly a decade and had displaced thousands of persons from their homes and into exile as refugees. Negotiations did not take place immediately. It was only after Nimeiri survived a left wing–backed coup attempt in 1971 and the Anyanya guerrillas had united under the leadership of Joseph Lagu that secret contacts between the government and Lagu's South Sudan Liberation Movement (SSLM) resulted in face-to-face negotiations in Addis Ababa in 1972 (Alier 1990, 49–95; Lagu 2006, 239–49; Poggo 2009, 169–87).

The Addis Ababa Agreement of 1972 was a compromise. The SSLM compromised by agreeing to the unity of Sudan; the government compromised by agreeing to establishing a semiautonomous southern region and absorbing Anyanya fighters into the national army. The Southern Regional Government was less than the federalism the SSLM and other political parties had advocated in that it did not extend to the rest of the country and left in place a strong central government (Alier 1990, 101–12; Lagu 2006, 252–55).

The peace agreement was widely welcomed by the civilian population of South Sudan. The strongest reservations came from within the exile movement and the Anyanya itself. It is important to recall, given later claims by Equatorian critics that the agreement had been a conspiracy between Dinka in the government and SSLM delegations, that the most vocal contemporary critics were exiles from Bahr el-Ghazal and Anyanya soldiers in Upper Nile (Alier 1990, 240–41; Arop 2006, 19–20, 25–26; Lagu 2006, 256–57).

During the lifetime of the Southern Regional Government, political factions developed around the old party competition of SANU and Southern Front, and between those who had remained inside Sudan ("insiders") and those who had left the country as exiles or refugees ("outsiders") during the war (Kasfir 1977). The insider/outsider disparity was never quantified because it was difficult to say just who belonged to which group. Many of the "outsiders" had not been actively involved in the armed struggle and had pursued their education as refugees, while many "insiders" had maintained surreptitious contact with the Anyanya and the exile movement. The perception of disparity fed into a new political divide between "Equatorians" and "Nilotics" (Wakason 1993; Badal 1994). Prior to independence most southerners employed in government or who formed the political class had been educated in schools in the agricultural districts of Equatoria and Bahr el-Ghazal. It was only in the late 1940s and early 1950s that a concerted effort had been made to enroll students from the two largest South Sudanese language groups, the Dinka and Nuer. The number of Dinka and Nuer employed in government jobs had been disproportionately low relative to their percentage of the population prior to independence. To many who were used to that disparity their increased numbers in the civil service, police, and army after 1972 seemed unnatural (Johnson 2011a, 51–53).

The survival of the Addis Ababa Agreement was based on an alliance between Nimeiri and South Sudanese against Nimeiri's northern opponents—especially the Umma, Democratic Union Party (DUP), and Islamic Charter Front (later renamed the National Islamic Front, NIF), who were committed to some form of a unitary Islamic state. This alliance lasted through two serious coup attempts in Khartoum in 1975 and 1976 but began to break apart with the 1977 "National Reconciliation," when Nimeiri brought his strongest northern opponents, including Sadiq al-Mahdi of the Umma and Hassan al-Turabi of the NIF, into government. Hardline opponents of the Addis Ababa Agreement were now in the central government and began the process of the Islamic reform of the Sudan's laws.

The 1979 confirmation of the discovery of large oil deposits within the north-south borderlands of Upper Nile and Southern Kordofan offered Sudan the prospect of finally escaping its underdevelopment and indebtedness. Paradoxically, it further undermined the stability brought by the Addis Ababa Agreement. Hassan al-Turabi's attempt in 1980 to have the national assembly redraw the Southern Region's borders to include its oil fields in Kordofan, though unsuccessful in the face of united southern opposition, contributed to South Sudanese political anxiety that Khartoum was determined to exclude the South from the oil industry (Badal 1986).

Nimeiri increasingly intervened in the politics of the Southern Region and supported the idea of redividing it into its three original provinces. Joseph Lagu proposed this idea to promote Equatorian particularism, resentful of the influence of leaders from Upper Nile and Bahr el-Ghazal in the Southern Regional Government, but it failed to get the backing of a majority in South Sudan, and even had considerable opposition in Equatoria. Nimeiri overrode this opposition when he unilaterally abrogated the Addis Ababa Agreement in May 1983 and divided the South into three weaker regions. The removal of the constitutional provisions embodied in the Addis Ababa Agreement enabled Nimeiri to introduce sharia law through the national assembly in September. By this time the civil war in the South had begun.

Two Wars

The official website of the Government of the Republic of South Sudan offers a summary of the country's
independence struggle from the Condominium to independence. "Sadly," it concludes, "37 of the past 56 years
have been wasted on major civil conflicts; the first from
1955–1972 and the second from 1983 to 2005 when the
Comprehensive Peace Agreement (CPA) was signed."
The government is not alone in giving such an extended
chronology of violent struggle, as academics, journalists, and politicians routinely refer to the first civil war as
having lasted for seventeen years, starting a few months
before national independence.[1]

This chapter provides a parallel look at the two
wars: their similarities and differences, their ideologies
and forms of mobilization, the involvement of other
countries, the creation of a new diaspora of the "Internally Displaced" in the north and refugee communities
abroad, and the role of the international oil industry in
ethnic cleansing and funding the war.

The 1955 Southern Disturbances

"Sudanization," a requirement agreed on by Britain and
Egypt before self-determination could take place, looked

less like national liberation to South Sudanese and more like recolonization. The vast majority of new administrators, police, and army officers who replaced British officials were northern Sudanese who, unlike their predecessors, had no previous experience in the South, no knowledge of local languages, and little knowledge of the people they were supposed to govern.

The tension this sudden changeover caused throughout South Sudan, the lack of any real stake in the new government that most South Sudanese had, and the uncertainties of the future created an explosive situation, especially in the rapidly developing western Equatorian towns of Nzara and Yambio and in the headquarters of the Equatorial Corps in Torit.

The mutiny that broke out in Torit in August 1955 was a local conspiracy with very little planning for a general rising. Other mutinies within the army, police, and prison service followed in Kapoeta, Juba, Terekeka, Yei, Meridi, Yambio, Nzara, and Malakal, but these were in response to the news from Torit rather than a coordinated rebellion. The mutineers had no clear objective: some wanted to delay the departure of the British, others wanted to unite with Egypt, and there was no strong demand for South Sudanese independence. The lack of organization and clear objectives of the mutiny meant it could not build on the widespread anxiety in the South and mobilize popular support. In Wau junior southern administrators led by police inspector Gordon Muortat Mayen persuaded senior northern officials to leave the province administration in their hands. In the 1960s Gordon Muortat would become a leading advocate for South Sudanese independence as president of the Nile Provisional Government, but in 1955 he helped keep his province quiet. The mutiny subsided after the arrival of reinforcements from the North, and the majority of mutineers fled to Uganda or into the bush.

In Khartoum al-Azhari and his government attributed the mutiny solely to Egyptian agitation to delay Sudanese independence. William Luce, the acting governor-general and former deputy governor of Equatoria province, had a more realistic understanding of events. The mutiny, he reported, was "symptomatic of the major internal political problem of the Sudan i.e. the relationship between the North and the South," which could be settled only by the Sudanese themselves. This would need "a re-appraisal (and it may be 'agonizing' for the Northern Sudanese) by all concerned . . . of the whole problem of building a stable, peaceful nation out of two such discordant elements regardless of North and South" (Johnson 1998c, 438–42, documents 396, 398).[2]

The First Civil War

Whether Sudanese parliamentarians seriously attempted an agonizing reappraisal, the military government of General Ibrahim Abboud that replaced them concluded that national unity could best be built around the twin principles of Arabism and Islam. Former southern parliamentarians were placed under political surveillance,

136

and South Sudanese civil servants, teachers, and students were visible targets of Arabization and proselytization. South Sudanese leaders were arrested or went into exile, schools were closed, and students, too, faced the choice of arrest or flight. Following widespread school strikes in the South in 1962, many students became refugees in neighboring countries, while others moved into the bush and joined the remnants of the 1955 mutineers (Poggo 2009, chap. 5; Akol 2005).

In the area around Torit following the mutiny there had been only sporadic hit-and-run raids by a combined group of mutineers and Lotuho monyomiji age-set warriors led by a dissident rain king, but this group disbanded after their leader's death in Uganda in 1960 (Simonse 1992, 312–13). Øystein Rolandsen has proposed that both a conducive environment and sustained leadership are needed to turn random acts of violence into a civil war. The environment was created by the increasingly repressive measures of the military regime, and the leadership was provided in the early 1960s by exiles and new recruits (Rolandsen 2011a, 2011b). These included former parliamentarians Joseph Oduho and Fr. Saturnino Lohure, civil administrators William Deng and Aggrey Jaden, trained military officers like Joseph Lagu, and student recruits like Samuel Gai Tut and Emmanuel Obuur Nhial, who became prominent leaders in the political and armed struggle. As the 1960s became a decade of political disappointment they were joined by other prominent figures such as Gordon

Muortat Mayen and Ezboni Mondiri (Wakason 1984, 184; Poggo 2009, chap. 3; Arop 2012, 89–99).

Political mobilization among exiles began around 1960, but both political and military organization proceeded slowly. The first exile political movement, SANU, named in imitation of the leading Kenyan and Tanganyikan nationalist parties, KANU and TANU, was formed in 1962. Recruitment into armed units proceeded at different paces in the three provinces, with recruits sent to training camps located near refugee settlements in Ethiopia, Congo, and the Central African Republic. Organized assaults on Sudanese army and police outposts by guerrilla units answering to the name of "Anyanya" (poison or snake venom) began in 1963. With no external political support and no source of supply, guerrilla units in the field at first tended to operate independently of each other. The overthrow of the military government in 1964 paradoxically gave the Anyanya their first real access to arms. The interim civilian government chose to support the Simba rebels in the Congo, but arms intended for the Simba fell into the hands of the Anyanya (Wakason 1984, 130–41, 157–58, 184–85).

Factionalism beset the southern guerrilla movements from the outset. SANU split over the failed 1965 Round Table Conference, with Joseph Oduho, Aggrey Jaden, and Fr. Saturnino Lohure forming an exile leadership. Over the next few years there were further splits and several attempts at forming "provisional governments" in the bush: the Azania Liberation Front, the

Anyidi Liberation Front, the Nile Provisional Government, the Nile Republic, even a Sueh River Republic. Sometimes these different groups clashed in the field. The leadership suffered other losses with the assassinations of Fr. Saturnino by the Sudanese and Ugandan armies in 1967 and of William Deng in 1968.

The early civil war was fought mainly along South Sudan's international borders, where the guerrillas had their bases. For most of the time there was no central military command; forces were organized provincially or subprovincially, with units operating mainly within their own localities. This limited territorial range was one of the movement's weaknesses, and only gradually did the Anyanya expand outside these areas and begin to overcome their factional differences.

From the mid-1960s civilians increasingly became targets of military operations. In 1965 the army carried out a series of massacres, in the largest of which, in Juba and Wau, many educated southerners were killed. The Anyanya advised people to move away from the roads, either by re-adopting the nineteenth-century deep rural strategy of relocating homesteads and farms away from the lines of communication or by becoming refugees in neighboring countries.

The Cold War intruded into Sudan's civil war with the 1967 Arab-Israeli War and the 1969 left-wing coup that brought in Ja'afar Nimeiri. The Soviet bloc substantially armed the Sudanese army, and Egypt and Libya assisted Khartoum with air power and trained personnel.

Israel took an interest in the Anyanya as a way of diverting Arab military resources. With assistance from Idi Amin of Uganda, Joseph Lagu won Israel's backing. As the conduit for military supplies he was able to bring the other Anyanya units under his command and supplant the exile politicians as leader of the movement, now renamed the Southern Sudanese Liberation Movement (SSLM).[3] This enabled him to present a strong front in the 1972 negotiations that ended the war.

The Outbreak of the Second Civil War

The conditions for a second civil war existed not just in the political discontent with the terms of the Addis Ababa Agreement and the performance of the Southern Regional Government but in the large body of persons with military and organizational experience gained in the previous war and the eleven years of relative peace that followed it. There had been a series of mutinies in Akobo (1975), Wau (1976), and Juba (1977) by Anyanya units dissatisfied with their integration into the Sudan Armed Forces (SAF). Many of the mutineers escaped to Ethiopia where, as a continuation of Cold War politics, they got support from the Derg regime in retaliation for Nimeiri's support for Eritrean and anti-Derg forces.

The mutineers called themselves Anyanya 2. It was a loose organization with broadly separatist aims. Those operating out of Ethiopia began making hit-and-run raids in 1980 and linked up with other disaffected groups inside the country, such as the Abyei Liberation

Front, formed by Ngok Dinka in Southern Kordofan in response to attacks by Misseriya Arabs supported by the army and police. As political tensions rose in the Southern Region over Nimeiri's move toward abrogating the Addis Ababa Agreement and imposing sharia law, Anyanya 2 attracted new recruits from army and police deserters and secondary school students, all of whom were channeled back to training camps in Ethiopia. They also established links with former Anyanya officers still in the army.

The flash point came at Bor on 16 May 1983, when the ex-Anyanya soldiers in Battalion 105 refused orders to be transferred to the north. After the battalion repulsed an attack by the Sudanese army, it met up with Anyanya 2 in the bush by prearrangement and headed for Ethiopia. Other mutinies soon followed in other parts of the South, and desertions accelerated. The Sudan People's Liberation Movement/Army (SPLM/A) was founded in July in Ethiopia out of the amalgamation of the Anyanya 2 and the new mutineers.[4]

There was an immediate conflict over goals and leadership. A younger group of Anyanya veterans that included John Garang, Kerubino Kuanyin Bol, Salva Kiir Mayardit, and William Nyuon Bany obtained the support of the Ethiopian government (then fighting a secessionist movement in Eritrea) by advocating the creation of a "New Sudan" based on a secular form of government, not secession for South Sudan. Samuel Gai Tut and Akwot Atem, senior and older Anyanya officers,

adhered to a southern secessionist platform and retained the loyalty of a number of Anyanya 2.

This split at the foundation of the SPLA meant that
it failed to create a united southern movement, and
fighting broke out between the SPLA and the mainly
Nuer adherents of Samuel Gai Tut. The SPLA was never
only a "Dinka army," but Nuer proximity to the Ethiopian border meant that fighting quickly degenerated
into a Nuer-SPLA fight. Khartoum then supported
disaffected Anyanya 2 remnants and transformed them
into the first of many tribal militias deployed to coun-
ter the SPLA's infiltration of the rural areas. There thus
was a strange collaboration between the supposedly
separatist Anyanya 2 being supplied by Khartoum to
fight the antiseparatist SPLA, a pattern that would be
repeated later in the war (Johnson and Prunier 1993;
Johnson 1998a).

The SPLA's national objective of a New Sudan enabled it to reach beyond South Sudan to other disaffected
regions. It carried the war outside the South into the ad-
jacent areas of the Blue Nile and Nuba Mountains. As
early as 1986 the war was no longer just a North-South
war, nor a Muslim-Christian war, nor even an Arab-
African war (James 2007; Johnson 2011a, 131–37). The
1987 truce between the SPLA and the Anyanya 2 led to
the incorporation of most of the Anyanya 2 into the
SPLA, giving the SPLA control of most of the rural areas
of the South. By early 1989 the SPLA had taken control
of many of the major towns of the region as well.

The overthrow of Nimeiri in 1985 was followed by a parliamentary government led by a coalition of the Umma Party, the DUP, and the National Islamic Front (NIF) under Sadiq al-Mahdi's premiership. Each of the parties was committed to some form of an Islamic constitution and was unwilling to engage with the SPLM's proposed New Sudan. As the country's economic condition worsened and the government's military position weakened, momentum for a negotiated peace increased within the coalition and the army. Early in 1989 Sadiq al-Mahdi finally agreed to negotiate mostly on the SPLM's terms of a secular state. There was no mention of self-determination for the South at this stage. The NIF-backed coup of Omar al-Bashir on 30 June 1989 ended any hope of negotiations, and fighting continued for another fifteen years.

The Split in the SPLA, 1991–2000

The SPLM's commitment to a united Sudan meant that it was able to form a common political front with the exiled northern opposition Sudanese parties gathered together under the umbrella of the National Democratic Alliance (NDA). But the civil wars in Ethiopia were also intensifying. Khartoum (with US support) backed the anti-Derg forces, while the SPLA became increasingly involved in supporting its patron, much to its cost, both militarily and politically.

At the beginning of 1991 the SPLA was on the verge of taking control of most of the South. The fall of the Derg in May deprived the SPLA of its bases, its supplies, and its support and left it vulnerable to a flanking attack through Ethiopia by the Sudanese army. The SPLA's policy of suppressing political dissent within the movement backfired by generating more opposition. In August 1991 Garang's leadership was challenged by two commanders in Nasir near the Ethiopian border, Riek Machar and Lam Akol, now left vulnerable by the collapse of their former Ethiopian ally.

The Nasir faction announced its goal to be the total independence of the South, but from the start it had the surreptitious support of Khartoum, who arranged a merger with the remaining Anyanya 2 militias. Fighting broke out in areas the SPLA had previously secured. Between 1993 and 1995 Khartoum was able to press the SPLA severely in Eastern Equatoria and the area between Juba and the Uganda border. But by 1995 Khartoum was isolated internationally when its former allies, Ethiopia and Eritrea, became alarmed about its political intentions in the region, and Uganda reacted to Khartoum's support for the Lord's Resistance Army. From 1996 to 1999 the SPLA regained much of its former position in the South, the Nuba Mountains, and Blue Nile. In alliance with the NDA it opened up another front in the eastern Sudan.

The Nasir faction failed to create a cohesive movement. The underlying contradiction of claiming to fight for the total independence of the South while collaborating with Khartoum could not be resolved.

The movement fractured and many of its commanders went back to the SPLA. To stop his support from haemorrhaging, Riek Machar made an open alliance with Khartoum in 1996–97, ostensibly committing Khartoum to allowing the South to vote, at some undetermined date in the future, on unity or independence. This did not stop the factionalism within the southern anti-Garang forces. Instead, factionalism intensified in a Nuer civil war fought for control of the western Upper Nile oil fields, with Riek Machar eventually rejoining the SPLM in 2002 (Johnson 2009c).

Khartoum used the Nuer splinter groups to open up the oil fields for exploitation, first with the aid of Canadian companies and then with substantial investment from China, other Asian countries, and Sweden (Large and Patey 2011). The new oil revenues increased Khartoum's military capability. The Sudan Armed Forces (SAF) developed a new strategy in the oil fields by combining air power with regular army units and militias on the ground in operations designed to depopulate strategic areas (Rone 2003). This strategy was adapted to other theaters as well, notably northern Bahr el-Ghazal, the Nuba Mountains, and, later, Darfur.

Security and the CPA

The regional Inter-governmental Authority for Development (IGAD) had begun hosting peace negotiations in 1993, but these had been moribund for many years. The US Bush administration brought a new commitment to supporting the IGAD talks after the 2001 9/11 attacks. In 2002 a separate ceasefire was established in the Nuba Mountains and peace talks were reconvened at Machakos, Kenya. The Machakos Protocol, signed on 20 July 2002, established the framework of the future peace agreement, committing both sides to the unity of the country, but granting the South the option of an independence referendum after an interim period. The agreement was between the government and the SPLM only. It applied to South Sudan and did not apply to Abyei, the Nuba Mountains, and Blue Nile where the SPLA was active. Neither the NDA nor any other regional opposition group was included.

The security protocol eventually agreed to in the Comprehensive Peace Agreement (CPA) provided for the removal of SAF from South Sudan and the transfer of SPLA units from the eastern Sudan back to the South. Theoretically, in the event of the South Sudanese referendum choosing unity a new national army was to be formed around the Joint Integrated Units (JIU), drawn equally from SAF and the SPLA. In practice, the SAF contingent was mainly composed of scarcely trained anti-SPLA militias, and the common complaint was that the JIUs were neither joint nor integrated. Some SPLA forces in Blue Nile and Southern Kordofan states were withdrawn while the rest remained as part of the JIU. Neither SAF nor the SPLA were stood down or demobilized during the interim period. All armed militias in the South were required to choose to join either SAF or the SPLA. In the 2006 Juba Agreement most chose to join the SPLA. Integrating them into the SPLA, while at the same time attempting to reduce overall numbers through Disarmament, Demobilization, and Reintegration (DDR) programs for individuals remained a challenge throughout the interim period, a task that was never fully completed, and would have serious security implications in the immediate aftermath of independence (LeRiche and Arnold 2012, 157–65).

Wars of Religion

Sudan's civil wars have been described as being fought between the "Christian and Animist South" and the "Arab and Muslim North." Religion has informed the decisions of leaders in both the North and the South. Educated South Sudanese drew inspiration from biblical parallels in formulating their political goals (Tounsel 2015). They opposed attempts to privilege Islam in the constitution in 1958, 1969, and 1983, on the grounds that this infringed religious freedom and relegated them to second-class citizenship. Government-sponsored construction of mosques and religious schools throughout South Sudan and the expulsion of Christian missionaries in 1964 convinced South Sudanese of the government's hostility to Christianity, and both the Anyanya and the SPLA received support from church groups (Hassan 2002; Gray 2002).

For some Muslim Sudanese leaders the confrontation with Christianity in South Sudan was more importantly a part of a global religious strategy. Imam Hadi al-Mahdi, shortly after leading a split in the Umma Party against his nephew Sadiq, declared on a visit to Saudi Arabia in 1965, "Sudan is, in its majority, an Islamic Arab country. *It constitutes the Islamic Arab spearhead in Africa, and the peaceful invading vanguard in the unexplored areas of Africa. For this reason Sudan is subjected to the enmity of the Crusaders and those who champion racism such as African nationalism.*" He went on to accuse the "Crusaders" and Israel of trying to create "an impregnable obstacle *to the civilized Arab invasion inside Africa*" (Anon. 1965, 6, italics in the original).

Sadiq al-Mahdi did not publicly align himself with this extreme Islamic project. During his first premiership in 1966 he advocated an alliance between Muslims and Christians to eliminate paganism in South Sudan "for humanitarian and humanistic purposes." In 1984, shortly before the overthrow of Nimeiri, he predicted the "inevitable" Islamization of South Sudan through the manipulation of political differences among its leaders and ethnic tensions among its people, and by Muslim scholars and merchants mixing with southerners "in a friendly way." During his second premiership his coalition allies in the DUP broadly supported this strategy (Johnson 2000b, 66–67).

Hassan al-Turabi's NIF, Sadiq al-Mahdi's other coalition ally, revived the global Islamization project. Turabi pushed for the incremental Islamization of Sudan's laws and constitution under both Nimeiri and

Table 8.1 Comparison of civil wars

First Civil War (1962–72)	Second Civil War (1983–2005)
Anyanya origins:	*SPLM/SPLA origins:*
- Failure of national self-determination process - Failure of parliamentary politics - Suppression by military government	- Failure of the Addis Ababa Agreement - Introduction of the September Laws - Alienation of land in the "marginal areas," particularly Nuba Mountains and Blue Nile
Anyanya theater of operations, recruitment and international support:	*SPLM/SPLA theater of operations, recruitment and international support:*
- 3 southern provinces - Army mutineers, students, civil servants, local recruitment to local units - Training camps in neighboring countries - Post-1967 equipment and limited training from Israel v. support for Khartoum from Egypt, Libya and the Soviet bloc	- 3 southern regions, Abyei, Nuba Mountains, southern Blue Nile, eastern Sudan - Ex-Anyanya in army, civil servants and politicians, students and youth, organized recruitment throughout the "liberated areas" and deployment throughout different war zones - Collaboration with other armed groups within the NDA (Sudan Alliance Forces, Eastern Front) - Support from Ethiopia and Uganda
Anyanya objective:	*SPLM objective:*
- Self-determination and independence for South Sudan alone	- "New Sudan" for entire country
Anyanya achievement:	*SPLM achievement:*
- Semiautonomous Southern Region within a united Sudan - Incorporation of Anyanya into national army	- Self-determination and independence for South Sudan - Retention of SPLA as a separate army - Promise of referendum in Abyei - Promise of "Popular Consultations" in South Kordofan and Blue Nile
Failure of the Addis Ababa Agreement:	*Failures of the CPA:*
- Abrogation of Addis Ababa Agreement and dissolution of the Southern Regional Government by presidential decree	- No general demobilization of all militaries - No process of South-South reconciliation - Abyei referendum aborted and Abyei occupied by Sudanese army - Failure of "Popular Consultations" and renewal of war in South Kordofan and Blue Nile

Sadiq. This enabled the SPLA to broaden its support and recruit Muslims who opposed the NIF's national project. Turabi's party proclaimed *jihad* against even Muslim opponents after seizing power in 1989. Turabi's attempt to create new Islamic Republics among Sudan's neighbors in the 1990s, especially within Ethiopia, finally led to Sudan's diplomatic isolation, the loss of its regional allies, and their realignment as allies of the SPLA, who remained committed to a nonsectarian "New Sudan."

9

Self-Determination in the Twenty-First Century

"It is obvious," the exile politician Oliver Albino (nick-named "the Old Fox") wrote in 1970, "that both the Arab North and the African South will have enormous advantages once they part in peace." Separation would bring stability to the North, which was as "disorganized and unable to maintain unity" as many new African states. The Southern state he envisaged would "include the Nuba, the Fur, and possibly the Ingesena [*sic*], who are an inalienable part of Southern Sudan, if the North is to be the stable, pure Arab state I have in mind." But first South Sudan should put its own house in order, "then we shall see what direction the political thoughts of the Africans in the North will take" (Albino 1970, 111).

Albino's ideal of two racially defined states, with South Sudan incorporating parts of Blue Nile, Kordofan, and Darfur, reemerged periodically over the next three decades as South Sudanese political thought alternated between ideas of federalism and self-determination. South Sudanese arguments developed within the context of postwar decolonization, in which the principles of self-government and self-determination as enunciated in the 1942 Atlantic Charter and the 1945 United Nations Charter were progressively redefined as anticolonial liberation (Healy 1983; Mayall 1983; Wiberg 1983).[1]

A Genealogy of South Sudanese Self-Determination

British administrators in Sudan did not immediately realize the implications of the Atlantic Charter. As late as 1945 the Sudan government restated the objective of Southern Policy as developing the southern provinces "on African and Negroid lines, and not upon the Middle Eastern and Arab lines," equipping the southern peoples "whether their future lot be eventually cast with the Northern Sudan or with East Africa (or partly with each)" (quoted in Collins 1983, 279). What distinguished "African and Negroid" from "Middle Eastern and Arab" lines was never fully defined. By the time the Juba Conference was convened in 1947, however, the government had abandoned any possibility of a separate arrangement for the southern provinces. The southern delegates were made aware of this change in policy only when the civil secretary, who chaired the meeting, asked if anyone objected to the unity of Sudan. "Chief Lapponya stated that the principle of unity could only be decided later when the Southerners were grown up, by which time they would be in a position to decide whether to join the North or go to the Belgian Congo or Uganda. The Chairman explained that people could not get up and go where they like just like that."[2]

The question of South Sudanese self-determination was thus subsumed in Sudanese self-determination, but the idea was dormant, not dead. The 1953 Self-Government Statute stipulated two sets of elections. The first would elect a self-governing parliament under a British governor-general to oversee Sudanization of the security services and civil administration and decide on a date for self-determination. The second would elect a constituent assembly in what would in effect be a self-determination referendum to choose between union with Egypt and independence. The constituent assembly would draft a constitution reflecting the outcome of the popular vote. The elections of 1953 produced a majority for the pro-Egyptian parties, who then formed the first government headed by Ismail al-Azhari.

The 1954 Juba Conference organized by Buth Diu and the Liberal Party advocated a federal system for South Sudan and the neighboring peoples of the Nuba Mountains, Darfur, and Blue Nile as well and confirmed that separation was the only alternative to a federal Sudan (Wawa 2005, 115–37). In affirming their own right to self-determination, Benjamin Lwoki, the conference chairman, declared, "As the South went into Parliament on [its] own will so it can choose to walk out of [it], last but not least we firmly believe in our right as [a] distinct race from the people of the Northern Sudan. We must determine to [*sic*] the future of the South in the way we think suits us or our aims" (Lwoki 1954).

The self-determination process was circumvented by a parliamentary vote, and the 1958 coup closed parliament and shut down any public constitutional debate. A new generation of former profederal leaders such as Fr. Saturnino Lohure and Joseph Oduho went into exile in neighboring countries just as they were achieving their own self-determination. South Sudanese exiles framed their aspirations in the new political language of African nationalism and pan-Africanism. SANU argued their case in terms of universal political rights and religious liberty in appeals to the UN and the newly created Organization of African Unity (OAU) and drew explicit parallels between Sudan under Arab rule and Africa under white rule, presenting themselves as part of an anticolonial struggle (SANU 1963). This shift in emphasis was a direct response to the UN's 1960 resolution that equated self-determination with anticolonialism but rejected separatism.[3]

When Sudan returned to multiparty democracy in 1964, this new anticolonial idiom became part of South Sudanese political discourse. Throughout the 1960s, internal and exile parties demonstrated a common understanding of their political past, presenting the South's history as being dominated by imperialists and neoimperialists, denying the constitutional validity of either the 1947 Juba Conference or the 1953 All Parties Agreement, and casting South Sudan's post-independence struggle in anticolonial and antiimperialist terms. For most South Sudanese, "self-determination" became a code word for "independence," as in Oduho and Deng's assertion, "We demand nothing short of self-determination, after which we shall be good friends" (Oduho and Deng 1963, 60).

In the 1972 Addis Ababa talks that ended the first civil war, the SSLM accepted the government's precondition of the principle of a united Sudan. The SSLM proposed a federal structure for the entire nation (SSLM 1972), but in the end negotiations focused on the details of the lesser option of regional autonomy for the South only. Self-determination as a process was abandoned, and the agreement was incorporated into the 1973 Permanent Constitution.

During its eleven-year existence (1972–83) the Southern Regional Government's autonomy was restricted by its subordination to the central government. The Southern Region, established without a popular mandate, was abolished by presidential decree in 1983. In the renewal of civil war the new South Sudanese guerrilla movement provided a different rationale and objective for its struggle.

How New Sudan Replaced Self-Determination and Self-Determination Replaced New Sudan

The SPLM/A was formed with the backing of socialist Ethiopia in July 1983. Its manifesto was broadly Marxist in tone, but its analysis of the failure of the Addis Ababa Agreement was rooted in debates that predated 1972. It offered a structural analysis of the Southern

Region's weaknesses and repudiated the idea that there was a "Southern Problem" that could be considered in isolation of the rest of the country. Its proposal of a restructured united Sudan reached back to the days of the federalist alliance between southern and regionalist parties in the 1958 and 1968 parliaments (SPLM 1983). This was more than a mere tactical move imposed on the SPLM by its Ethiopian backers, because the movement retained this basic principle even as it shed its Marxist language following the overthrow of the Mengistu regime in 1991.

The SPLM presented itself as a national organization, but it remained at heart a South Sudanese movement in which separatist sentiment remained strong, if latent, among the rank and file. The NIF coup of 1989 brought an end to the constitutional discussions between the SPLM and the parliamentary government. The NIF's open pursuit of the Islamist agenda strengthened separatist sentiment among South Sudanese, and the SPLM was preparing a position on self-determination in 1991 when the collapse of the Mengistu government in Ethiopia precipitated a coup attempt within the SPLM/A itself.

General Ibrahim Babangida of Nigeria, then president of the OAU, hosted peace talks between the NIF government and the two SPLM factions at Abuja in 1992. Garang's SPLM restated its objective of a secular state but qualified this by declaring that should the Khartoum government remain adamantly committed to an

Islamic state, the South and other "marginalized areas" should exercise their own right for self-determination, with independence as an option (SPLM 1992). The SPLM delegates were under pressure from the Nigerian government and OAU observers to formulate a united negotiating position. The delegations merged and issued a joint statement, committing themselves not only to championing "the right of the peoples of Southern Sudan to self-determination," but affirming "the wishes of the people of Abyei, the Nuba mountains and southern Blue Nile, shall likewise be expressed through the process of self-determination together with the south" (SPLM/SPLA 1992). The joint declaration did not lead to a reunification of the SPLM, nor even to a lessening of conflict between the factions. But it did put the principle of self-determination—for the South as well as other regions of Sudan—back into public circulation as a method of ending the war.

The right of self-determination was reaffirmed in a series of subsequent negotiations and declarations. The round of negotiations initiated by the IGAD governments in 1994 included self-determination through a referendum as the basis on which negotiations between the government and the SPLM should take place in their Declaration of Principles. The 1995 Asmara Declaration, signed by the umbrella opposition National Democratic Alliance, also recognized the right of self-determination for the South and other areas. The 1997 Khartoum Agreement between Riek Machar's SPLM faction and the NIF government promised South Sudan only an independence referendum in the undisclosed future, and this was incorporated in the constitution of the same year. Together these documents committed the Sudan government and all the main northern Sudanese opposition parties to recognizing some form of self-determination as a means of ending the war.

The definition of who would be granted self-determination would determine the limits of that self-determination. The SPLM's "marginalized areas" was a coded term for "African" areas outside South Sudan's administrative boundaries: the Dinka of Abyei, the Nuba of Southern Kordofan, and the peoples of southern Blue Nile. But in the mid-1990s the SPLA opened new fronts in other northern areas, and for the first time such dissident northern groups as the Beja Congress had a military presence in the country in active opposition to Khartoum. The SPLM's definition of the right of self-determination theoretically extended to them, too, but on what terms?

National identity and religious freedom were only two of the issues over which the war was being fought. The control of resources was closely linked to national identity. The struggle for control of oil in the South was paralleled by a more insidious and less well-publicized struggle for land and labor in the eastern Sudan, Blue Nile, Southern Kordofan, Darfur, and even Nubia around the projected Merowe Dam. The Islamist military government in Khartoum did more than any previous government to accelerate asset transfer. Adapting colonial land registration laws, the Khartoum government transferred land from common resource use first to government and then to private ownership. Using the instruments of state and international Islamic financial institutions, the government systematically transformed many rural areas of northern Sudan into a patchwork of large mechanized estates, owned and controlled by the government's internal allies or international backers, and often worked by a new dispossessed, war-displaced rural proletariat. For this reason, calls for self-determination within these "marginalized regions" concentrated on the protection of local rights and did not support new separatist movements. The resurrection of self-determination in these areas stemmed directly from the failure of self-determination for Sudan at independence, and referred back to the unfinished constitutional business of 1956.

Peace negotiations were restarted in 2002 with the involvement of US President Bush's envoy for Sudan, Senator John C. Danforth. The SPLM was still officially committed to replacing the Islamist regime with a secular "New Sudan" run by the SPLM and the northern opposition. Failing that, the next best solution was replacing the old unitary Sudan with a loose confederation through a "constitutional separation" between North and South. If these two options were impossible to achieve, then self-determination leading to the total independence of the South was the final option.[4]

The United States' initial position expressed by its special envoy clearly discouraged any such third option. His report to President Bush in April 2002 dismissed both the SPLM's other two options, proposing, instead, a unitary Sudan with an Islamic state in the North and a resurrected regional government in the South, protected by vague guarantees for political, religious, and civil rights (Danforth 2002).

The US State Department proposed to table a draft text of an agreement that followed the Danforth report's recommendations, leaving the Khartoum regime in control of the whole of the North, and offering South Sudan a weak regional government. The SPLM were denied either their first or their second objectives, leaving them with the choice either of surrendering or of going for their final option, self-determination for South Sudan alone. The Machakos Protocol agreed by the two parties in July 2002 proclaimed unity as the objective framework for future talks, but accepted self-determination with the possibility of independence as the fail-safe option for the South. Because Danforth failed to offer any realistic proposals for obtaining the equal citizenship rights the SPLM favored, his attempt to exclude secession from the negotiations served only to elevate it among the SPLM's priorities, making it the only viable option to a unitary state dominated by the ruling National Congress Party (NCP).

Self-determination for the South alone did not resolve the issue of self-determination for other areas in rebellion. There were many more diverse combatants in 2002 than there had been in 1983, fighting for different immediate objectives. Ultimately what South Sudanese had in common with the Nuba of South Kordofan, the peoples of the southern Blue Nile, and the non-Arab Muslims of Darfur and the eastern Sudan was a desire for a more economically and politically just country. But an independent South Sudan would not, by itself, solve the problems confronting those other regions that were a part of the conflict.

The SPLM insisted on reinserting the three marginalized areas of Abyei, Blue Nile, and the Nuba Mountains as separate topics when talks resumed. Khartoum saw this as diluting the Islamic state in the North. South Sudanese critics objected that inclusion of the marginalized areas delayed and jeopardized the South's self-determination. With such resistance the protocols on the three areas in the CPA were the last to be agreed on in 2004.

Garang's answer to critics and skeptical supporters alike was to emphasize self-determination as a process, not as an objective in itself. He still maintained that a united Sudan, based on universal ideals of humanity, was possible, and could be achieved if all the protocols of the CPA were fully implemented. But if it didn't work, "other solutions are available," and Sudan could split into two, or more, countries. The only real choice, he said, was between a transformed Sudan and an independent South Sudan; South Sudanese would have to decide whether what was started by the peace agreement would lead to that transformation. As for the Nuba Mountains and Blue Nile, he admitted that a compromise of "popular consultation," falling short of the right of self-determination, had been reached in the setting up of state parliaments in those two regions. But this was to be a democratic process, and just as independence came to the Sudan through a vote of parliament, the same could happen in the state parliaments of the Nuba Mountains and Blue Nile.[5]

Unity in Principle and Practice

The CPA stipulated that the choice presented to South Sudanese in the referendum would be between unity under "the system of government established under the Peace Agreement" and independence, but it also stipulated that both parties were "to make the unity of the Sudan an attractive option especially to the people of South Sudan." Independence might have been hypothetical, but unity was not. South Sudanese might not have been certain of what independence would bring, but they knew what unity had brought them and what unity under the existing system of government had to offer.

The arguments in favor of unity were mainly practical. No geological fault would divide the South from the North after the referendum, so there was a need to facilitate the movement of peoples and goods between the two regions, to manage natural resources, particularly oil and water, and to attract investment. All of these are theoretically best managed within a united country rather than between two countries.

The South Sudanese experience of actual as opposed to theoretical unity, however, had been ambiguous. Government in Sudan has been highly centralized since independence, and participation in it by groups outside the central Nile valley had been limited (JEM 2004). Central government appointed local authorities and set administrative, educational, development, and investment policies and budgets. Political agreements were unilaterally set aside by central governments of all northern parties, resulting in two civil wars (Alier 1990). The movement of peoples was not always free: labor had been dispossessed either by development policies in which land was alienated for national development projects or by war, and sometimes by war as a means of promoting national development policies (Kibreab 2002, 272–80; Duffield 1992, 50–51; Moro 2008). The tenure of dispossessed persons displaced to the towns was also insecure: there had been mass expulsions of South Sudanese residents from the national capital by Nimeiri's government, and the NCP regime routinely demolished the shanties of displaced persons in their settlements around the capital.

The CPA was supposed to establish a system of government that would correct the imbalances of the past. The SPLM's New Sudan project at least articulated the movement's idea of what would "make the unity of the Sudan an attractive option especially to the people of

South Sudan." The NCP made no explicit commitment beyond the generalities of the CPA.

South Sudanese ministers and civil servants appointed to the Government of National Unity (GoNU) complained that they were ineffective and irrelevant because the civil service was controlled by the NCP. With a built-in majority in the National Assembly established by the CPA, NCP parliamentarians often attempted to alter agreements negotiated with the SPLM, attempting, for instance, to alter the 2009 referendum law. The NCP's postelection majority was even bigger, and the assembly attempted to delay the referendum process further in its rejection of the presidency's nomination of referendum commissioners.

Many South Sudanese saw the nonimplementation of major provisions of the CPA as acts of bad faith on the part of the NCP. The controversy over Abyei was the starkest example. Whereas both sides signed up to accept the Abyei Boundary Commission's report as "final and binding," the NCP immediately repudiated it. Both sides again agreed to implement immediately the 2009 boundary determined by the Permanent Court of Arbitration in The Hague, but SAF prevented demarcation. There were additional delays over the definition of the North-South boundary and some attempts by NCP members of the government to try to use that disagreement to delay the referendum. These examples reminded many southerners of the dishonored agreements of previous regimes.

Self-Determination in the Border Areas

Muslims as well as non-Muslims from the Nuba Mountains and Blue Nile had joined the war to fight against political and economic marginalization, but neither region was adequately catered for in the peace agreement. The "popular consultation" provided for at the end of the interim period was limited in scope. The state legislatures were to assess the implementation of the CPA in their states, and after such a review should either of the legislatures "decide to rectify, within the framework of the Agreement, any shortcomings in the constitutional, political and administrative arrangements of the Agreement, then such legislature shall engage in negotiations with the National Government with the view of rectifying these shortcomings."[6]

There were few in the SPLM hierarchy who were willing to push forward an agenda for these marginalized populations on the national stage after Garang's death in July 2005. The SPLM's confused approach to elections in the North in April 2010 left Blue Nile with an SPLM governor but an NCP majority in the state legislature. The legislature rejected the demand for greater autonomy that had emerged from the statewide popular meetings convened by the governor. Southern Kordofan's elections were delayed until June 2011, after the southern referendum. By the time the state legislature ratified the existing administrative arrangements Khartoum had resumed war against SPLM-North in Southern Kordofan, and SPLM-North was no longer represented in the assembly. President Bashir had already decided what the outcome of the political process would be. Following the southern referendum he declared that Sudan had finally determined its identity. In a distorted echo of Oliver Albino's vision of racially determined states, he proclaimed that there would be no question of cultural or ethnic diversity. Popular consultation did not include any radical renegotiation of the CPA, nor did it include the option of either state joining South Sudan, contrary to Garang's 2004 pronouncement. The resumption of war in Sudan's "new south" killed off the prospect of self-determination in the border regions.

After resumption of war in Sudan's southern borderlands and the outbreak of civil war in South Sudan, it became fashionable among many international commentators to blame neoliberal peacemakers in the West, the US government in particular (but even Hollywood actors), for precipitating a premature independence for South Sudan (Young 2012). This emphasis on external agents ignored the long history of the idea of self-determination in South Sudanese political thought, where a consistent theme was that the unity of Sudan must be based on equality: equality in citizenship rights, equality in the exercise of political power, and equality in the access to and benefits of resources—an equality Sudan has yet to attain for all its citizens. South Sudanese were asked to make a long-term choice about their future in the referendum. The choice was not a referendum on the governing party, but on how South Sudanese would govern themselves now and in the future. Given more than half a century's experience of Sudanese unity, the result was never in doubt. In January 2011 South Sudanese voted overwhelmingly for independence, the only Sudanese people so far to have exercised the popular right of self-determination.

10

Legacies of War

During London's 2012 Cultural Olympiad the newly formed South Sudan Theatre Company performed Shakespeare's *Cymbeline* in the vernacular of Juba Arabic at the Globe Theatre to enthusiastic reviews. The play depicts a small nation standing against a stronger military power's demand for tribute while its court is undermined by intrigue, treason, betrayal, and rape. Its production coincided with the eruption of fighting along the Sudan–South Sudan border centered on the disputed Panthou/Heglig oil field as the comprehensive peace began to look like a brief truce within a longer war. "When we read this man Shakespeare," the play's translator and codirector explained, "we think he was writing about us. We can see all our problems and stories are in the play" (Wynne-Jones 2012).

South Sudan achieved cultural visibility with nationhood. Prior to its independence no southern Sudanese theater company would have represented Sudan in an international festival. It is part of a trend: South Sudanese football teams compete internationally, South Sudanese women represent their nation in international beauty pageants, and South Sudanese athletes, actors, musicians, and models appear in Western media. A celebration of South Sudanese cultural vitality, the production of *Cymbeline* acknowledged South Sudan's uncertain future, serial defections by its political and military leaders, and its history of gendered violence. It was a prescient choice, but in highlighting the inward-looking self-interest of political actors it also demonstrated an outward-looking resilient creativity gained from surviving the experiences of war and displacement.

It is fitting for a longue durée history to end by looking at the future, at those external and internal factors that promote either instability or stability. Most of the threats to stability at independence stemmed from the failures of the CPA and the legacies of war. The CPA resolved Sudan's longest-standing political question: whether or not South Sudanese would find a place within the Sudanese nation. It did not resolve the equally pressing problem of the state's relations with its other marginalized peripheries. Nor did it provide a blueprint for a peaceful disengagement between Sudan and South Sudan, or for any process of reconciliation between communities affected by the war. The first years of South Sudan's independence were marked by continued tension with Sudan, violence along their common border, and a crisis of governance and insecurity within South Sudan. Yet the new nation also possessed assets with the potential for resolving conflict and rebuilding the nation.

External Challenges to Stability

South Sudan's independence was accompanied by renewed war along Sudan's "new south." The issue of the
disputed territory of Abyei remained unresolved. Armed
groups prevented a referendum being held to decide
whether it would remain part of Sudan or join South
Sudan. SAF occupied it just two months before South
Sudan's formal independence. The northern members of
the SPLM and SPLA based in the Nuba Mountains and
Blue Nile were separated from the SPLM in South Sudan,
and war resumed in those two areas when SAF attacked
SPLM-North officials and SPLA-North units in South
Kordofan in June 2011 and in the Blue Nile in September.

Sudan's internal wars were clustered mainly along
South Sudan's border, from South Darfur through
Southern Kordofan and Blue Nile. The UN Mission
in Sudan and other agencies documented numerous
violations of human rights and international humanitarian laws by government forces in Abyei, the Nuba
Mountains, and Blue Nile during the fighting in 2011
(SHRM 2011; UNMIS 2011; Rottenburg, Komey, and
Ille 2011; ICG 2013a, 2013b). Civilians in both Blue
Nile and the Nuba Mountains continued to be attacked
on the ground and from the air. Thousands of refugees
fled into Unity and Upper Nile states in South Sudan,
while the Sudanese air force bombed refugee camps
there. The new war was replicating the patterns of the
previous wars (Amnesty International 2013, 2015; De
Alessi 2015).

South Sudan is inevitably affected by what happens along its border with Sudan. By 2005 the SPLA had a strong military presence along South Sudan's northern boundary and territorial claims north of the official boundary line stipulated by the CPA. Both Juba and Khartoum supported each other's armed opposition along this common border, but the fighting in Sudan's new south was not a proxy war between the two countries. The CPA had denied the peoples of Blue Nile and the Nuba Mountains their right to self-determination by subordinating that right to South Sudan's. Freed from the dominance of South Sudanese priorities the SPLA-North was able to form its own alliances with other Sudanese opposition groups, linking up with such Darfur forces as the Justice and Equality Movement (JEM), who expanded their own operations into South and North Kordofan. South Sudan remains vulnerable to external threats from across the border until a just and sustainable peace ends Sudan's internal wars.

The main unresolved border issues are the disputed territories of the mineral-bearing Hofrat en-Nahas/Kafia Kingi district, the "Mile 14" region between the Malual Dinka and Rizeigat Baggara, the Panthou/Heglig oil fields between South Kordofan and Unity states, and Abyei (Johnson 2009b, 2010, 2012; Vaughan, Schomerus, and De Vries 2013). Many of these territorial disputes had their origins in Condominium-era decisions. The area of western Bahr el-Ghazal containing Kafia Kingi and the copper mines of Hofrat en-Nahas was considered to be a remote district and a cultural and religious border zone. A renewed interest in the mineral potential around Hofrat en-Nahas led to its transfer to Darfur in 1960, a transfer that was supposed to be reversed by the Addis Ababa Agreement but never was. The territories of "Mile 14" and Panthou/Heglig contain disputed grazing areas, and South Sudan's case rests on the claims of its pastoralists. The area of Abyei, the home of the Ngok Dinka, has similarities with all three territories. As with Kafia Kingi it is unfinished business left over from the Addis Ababa Agreement when a promised referendum on joining the Southern Region was never held. As with "Mile 14," its ownership is disputed between competing Baggara and Dinka pastoralists, and as with Panthou/Heglig, the presence of oil sharpened the competing claims of Khartoum and Juba. Successive regimes in Khartoum have attempted the demographic transformation of the area by settling Baggara in Ngok Dinka territory (F. Deng 1986; Cole and Huntingdon 1997; Johnson 2008; 2011c; Craze 2014).

South Sudan and Sudan share considerable economic interests along the borderlands, and the disputed territories are among those where these interests are at their most dense. Yet both governments were willing to damage their own economies in order to hurt each other in 2012 when South Sudan temporarily shut down its pipelines to Port Sudan, the only means of exporting its oil, and Sudan retaliated by closing the border to all trade. Repeated tensions created a very real apprehension of renewed war with Sudan.

Security issues dominated South Sudan's relations with Sudan, delaying resolutions to the border, oil fees, and Abyei. Relations thawed with agreements in 2013 to cease supporting each other's armed opposition, but the impact of that thaw on South Sudan's internal politics helped precipitate the political crisis at the end of that year. Officials hostile to Khartoum were dismissed from government and party posts and replaced by persons with a more flexible attitude, some of them former NCP members. South Sudan's national security service became more active against internal political dissent. These moves exacerbated South Sudan's internal governance crisis.

Crisis of Governance and the Challenges of Internal Instability

South Sudan's postwar crisis of governance was more than just the problem of converting a guerrilla movement into a civil government. The death of John Garang three weeks into the interim period created a crisis of leadership within the SPLM that was never fully resolved. The new president, Salva Kiir Mayardit, failed to control the factions that developed within the party, impose accountability, and rein in corruption (Nyaba 2011). The uncertainties of the interim period, given the constant possibility of a reversal back to war with Khartoum, inhibited the much-needed transformation.

Reform of the SPLA into a professional army was put on hold as priority was given to absorbing semitrained former government militias, with their largely illiterate commanders, into the SPLA. Reform of SPLM into a fully functioning political party halted as political attention focused on the 2011 independence referendum.

South Sudan inherited from Sudan's constitution a ten-state semifederal administrative system dependent on central government funding. The existing bureaucracy had to be merged with the SPLM/A's wartime administration, resulting in a bloated salary commitment in the government budget. A lack of financial accountability within the SPLA during the war years carried over into government. Oil revenues, which formed the majority of government income, disappeared into private accounts (de Waal 2014). During the war, senior SPLA commanders accumulated wealth in trade and cattle and were able to expand their patronage by providing their soldiers with bridewealth cattle. After 2005, government officials at various levels were able to service these patronage networks with cash rather than cattle. This was often the only social welfare safety net available to SPLA veterans and civilians affected by war (Pinaud 2013, 129–35).

Land policy has the potential to create popular discontent. The insecurity of tenure in urban areas has received most attention, particularly in the national capital of Juba where land-grabbing and land evictions were common. Politicians, SPLA officers, and state security officials were most commonly identified as the main culprits in acquiring land by illegal means (D. Deng 2014c), but in fact most evictions and demolitions were instigated by the Central Equatoria state government rather than by individuals in the SPLM (Badiey 2014). Corruption involved in the sale or leasing of rural land has a far greater potential to arouse political opposition and insurgency. By 2014, 8.4 percent of South Sudan's total land area, some 5.18 million hectares, had been acquired by foreign as well as South Sudanese investors, mostly on community land without the knowledge of the local communities. Two of the states most affected are Jonglei and Unity, also the two states most affected by civil war after 2013 (D. Deng 2015).

South Sudan's postindependence transitional constitution entrenched the power of the executive and the SPLM. The SPLM was both the majority and the ruling party, but post-2011 South Sudan was a multiparty state with minority parties represented in the national and state legislatures as well as in the cabinets of the central and state governments. Within the SPLM there was resistance to internal change and constitutional reform. The government of South Sudan began to resemble those aspects of the Khartoum regime the SPLM had repeatedly repudiated: the concentration of power in the office of the president, interference in the administration of the states by the central government, and impunity of an increasingly arbitrary state security service.

The unresolved issues of the SPLM and SPLA converged in 2013, coming to a head over the preparations for the 2015 presidential election. Within the top leadership of the SPLM there was a large constituency in favor of reform and a specific challenge by the vice president, Riek Machar, for the party's nomination for president. Machar openly wooed Nuer constituencies, some connected to former government militias, speaking to their sense of entitlement and bolstering his campaign with bogus prophecies. The president's dismissal of the vice president, the entire cabinet, and many SPLM officials in July 2013 drove the reform coalition into an uneasy alliance with Machar, and this confrontation led to an outbreak of violence in Juba on 15 December 2013. The president alleged that a coup had been attempted and unleashed a personal bodyguard, which was separate from the SPLA, into the largely Nuer neighborhoods of Juba. Riek Machar escaped to Jonglei, where he met up with the former Nuer militias within the SPLA and called for the overthrow of the government. Jonglei was already the epicenter of postwar violence, and the civil war quickly escalated.

Internal Insecurity

One of the contributing factors to South Sudan's postindependence crisis was the government's failure to use the six-year interim period before the independence referendum to confront directly the internal wounds of the civil war and promote reconciliation between South Sudanese communities. There was no active program of reconciliation and compensation at the community level. Civilian communities throughout South Sudan had been subject to attacks by opposed armies and allied militias and recruitment into armed forces. Jonglei had been the recruiting ground for government-backed Nuer and Murle militias, and both Jonglei and Unity became the main battlefields in the conflict between the SPLA and Riek Machar's fragmenting faction in the 1990s (Mawson 1991; Johnson 2009c; Thomas 2014, chap. 7). The legacy of wartime violence had a serious effect on social relations within war-affected civilian communities, especially for women and youth.

A geography of violence saw some areas alternating between peaks of violence and relative peace. The increase in the violence against women was linked to the increase in the violence against noncombatants (Pinaud 2013, 95–99, 123–29). Young men were subject to conscription by the SPLA and competing militias, or targets of government counterinsurgency programs that saw them as potential rebel recruits. Armed and introduced to a brutal gun culture through military training and political indoctrination, many young men were no longer controlled by the social restraints of family and community (Leonardi 2007; Pinaud 2013, 117–27; Thomas 2014, 187–89). In some societies the new military institutions replaced or altered the older age-set systems. Among the Nuer of Upper Nile and Jonglei the formal initiation of boys into named age-sets by their elders ceased to be a universal practice. In the early years of the war the SPLA discouraged the formation of age-sets, sometimes co-opting historic age-set names, such as Koryom ("Locust"), for their own battalions (Stringham 2016). With the fragmentation of the SPLA in the Nuer areas during the 1990s, however, youth increasingly took control of their own ad hoc military organizations, the *bunam,* which almost entirely replaced the age-sets. The Murle used their more hierarchical age-set system for recruiting into the government-backed militias. As the war continued, the need for younger recruits led to a shrinking of the age range between age-sets, with junior age-sets challenging the authority of senior sets (Thomas 2014, 194–202). In Eastern Equatoria, too, junior age-sets sometimes displaced elder ones by gaining seniority through mass enlistment in the SPLA (Kurimoto 1994, 107–8; Simonse 1998, 73).

Jonglei had seen some of the worst fighting between the SPLA factions in the 1990s as well as raids on civilian communities by government militias. Civilians armed themselves in self-defense. After 2005 the government of South Sudan attempted peacemaking through heavy-handed disarmament campaigns which only fueled further resentment and rearmament and contributed to the continuation of civilian militia activity, often surreptitiously armed by Khartoum. This led to an explosion of violence between 2007 and 2013, mainly between the Lou Nuer and the Murle as bunam youth groups took the initiative in rearming and retaliating against Murle cattle raids, and the revived Murle militia under new leadership recruited Murle youth to fight both the Nuer and the government. With very little internal development in the state and few livelihoods available other than the cattle culture, youth had many incentives for participating in the livelihood offered by expanded raiding (Thomas 2014, chaps. 8–9). Civilians on both sides were subjected to new levels of brutality. Jonglei's organized armed civilian groups were ready recruits for an antigovernment insurgency.

Revenge killings followed immediately after the Juba violence as armed groups of Nuer attacked Dinka and other civilians in Akobo, Bor, Malakal, and Bentiu, despite their lack of involvement in the slaughter in Juba. Fighting between government and opposition forces continued throughout 2014 and 2016, often targeting mainly civilians. The number of persons killed remains unconfirmed.[1] What has been confirmed is the figure of nearly 2 million persons displaced, over 1.4 million internally and nearly half a million as refugees to neighboring countries (Amnesty International 2014; African Union 2014; SSHRC 2014; UNMISS 2014a, 2014b, 2014c, 2015; OHCHR 2015).

After the SPLM's internal political confrontation erupted into violence in December 2013 there was a gradual convergence of Sudan and South Sudan's civil wars. While professing support for Juba, Khartoum helped arm the opposition forces. Khartoum's opposition—JEM in particular—allied with Juba in combating the advance of the opposition forces into Upper Nile and Unity states. Thus the two civil wars intertwined (ICG 2015).

The IGAD-sponsored negotiations in Addis Ababa received strong international support. A peace agreement focusing on power sharing and the distribution of offices was signed in 2015. But considering the differing goals of the political and military opposition leaders (Young 2015) and several violations of the cease-fire, much more than power sharing will be needed to bring peace to the nation.

Forces for Stability, Peacemaking, and Reconciliation

Shortly after the African Union released its report on violence in South Sudan, one member of the diaspora posted on social media the comment, placed on record by the report, "that we all lost our humanity. . . . But that is a fact we can acknowledge in hope that we can change." Whatever agreements are reached, the prospects for a stable peace depend on the wider society. There are signs for hope in the failure of ethnic mobilization, the rising interest in promoting some form of federal governance, the experience of South Sudanese in local-level peacemaking as the foundation on which to build transitional justice, and the actions of some returning diaspora.

Despite the ethnic character of the first few months of the war, South Sudanese as a whole did not respond to attempts at ethnic mobilization. Retired politicians formed themselves into ethnic councils—the Jieng [Dinka] Council of Elders, and the Nuer Council of Elders—which while loosely affiliated with the government or the opposition have yet to demonstrate any substantial popular support. There are Nuer fighting on the government side and Nuer still working in government in Juba and the war-affected states. There are Dinka in the opposition and others who have refused to align themselves with either side. The theater of war remained largely confined to Unity, Jonglei, and parts of Upper Nile, despite localized rebellions elsewhere. The opposition's initial appeal to a sense of Nuer grievance and Nuer entitlement offered other South Sudanese few incentives to join a unified movement. There were revenge killings and outbreaks of opportunistic violence outside the main theaters of war (UNHRC 2016), but no popular mobilization of all against all.

The rupture in the SPLM has at least widened the discussion of the constitutional future for the nation, opening up a public debate about the options between the "decentralized" structure inherited from the CPA and some form of federalism. Federalism became the preferred system for many, though with no agreed definition of the form it should take. For some, "federalism" became a code word for ethnic particularism. Both the opposition and the government adopted top-down forms of federalism with new states decreed by executive order, entrenching an ethnically balkanized nation (Johnson 2014). There has been a demand for wider constitutional consultations to promote a more rigorous examination of the pros and cons of federal systems, with a clearer definition of the division of powers between a federal government and the states.

South Sudanese have a history of local peacemaking. The procedures and rituals are well known throughout

South Sudan, and in the immediate aftermath of war had some encouraging successes, such as the formal peace between the Malual Dinka of Northern Bahr el-Ghazal and the Rizeigat and Misseriya that allowed the Baggara to renew their seasonal use of Dinka grazing (Santschi 2009; PASS 2010). The universal experience of the role customary courts and intertribal meetings play in local government, a kind of second-tier federalism, can be the basis on which a broader form of transitional justice, reconciliation, and healing at the community level can be built (D. Deng 2014a, 2014b; SSLS 2015).

It is here that the South Sudanese diaspora is beginning to make the positive impact denied diasporans by their general exclusion from government and administration. In the first civil war the diaspora were found mainly as refugees in neighboring countries, some remaining in their host countries long beyond the signing of peace. The return of such refugees from Uganda after the fall of Idi Amin fed into the "insider/outsider" controversy about who was entitled to a government job. The diasporans created by the second civil war had a much more varied experience: some in refugee camps in Ethiopia, Kenya, and Uganda (e.g., Falge 2016); others as asylum seekers and resettled refugees in Europe, Australia, and North America; and a substantial number as "Internally Displaced Persons" in northern Sudanese cities. Each had a different set of experiences and opportunities. By the early 1990s, for instance, displaced South Sudanese made up more than a third of the population of Khartoum, and their experience there as unwanted outsiders helped promote a South Sudanese identity that transcended ethnic identities (F. Ibrahim 1991).

The return of the diaspora has not been without its problems in a renewed "insider/outsider" division. Those who have returned with education and skills acquired abroad have often found government positions reserved for SPLM/A veterans. Returning diaspora from Khartoum who were educated in Arabic have found obstacles to their integration into the English school curriculum or the English-language civil administration.

The diaspora involvement in the postindependence crisis has been mixed. Some of the most extreme exhortations to violence were posted on diaspora websites, which also circulated distorted and unsubstantiated reports whose main purpose can only have been to inflame political passions. Yet other diasporans have been involved in local-level community projects, such as the promotion of primary schools and girls' education, or have started small businesses. The crisis also revealed the vitality of a number of new civil society organizations and the wide range of expertise they draw on from the diaspora and across the regional and ethnic divisions within the nation. Many of the civil society organizations have produced thorough and well-reasoned proposals for the country escaping its current crisis. The diaspora have even managed to bring political satire to South Sudan through the website "Saakam!"—literally "What time?," but as an expression of incredulity can be broadly translated as "Say What?"—South Sudan's answer to America's *The Onion* and Britain's *Private Eye* (motto: "Sharing news like it never happened, making you think like you count"). It has highlighted the dilemmas of the political actors through fake headlines such as "SPLM to tighten membership rules, making resignation harder but more profitable," "Kenya regrets 'teaching' South Sudan corruption," "Vatican to lend 'Popemobile' for Machar's Juba visit," and "New S Sudan states run out of new symbols, clash over old ones." Some of its stories, such as the report of the merging of the Jieng and Nuer Councils of Elders, have been mistaken for genuine news reports and picked up by other websites, and the government had to deny that the president had endorsed Donald Trump in the US presidential race when a Saakam story went viral. Within all these activities lies some hope, if not for the immediate future, then for the long-term future of the country.

Political turmoil is a theme that recurs in indigenous oral traditions, as in the myth of the spear and the bead described in chapter 2. Now more than ever South Sudanese need reminding of the common moral theme of that cycle of myths: "that getting your very own back, a kind of reciprocation without exchange, leads to the permanent alienation of neighbours so that they can never again live together as members of the same community" (Lienhardt 1975, 216).

Notes

Chapter 4: Trade and Empires, Tribal Zones and Deep Rurals

1. See Hill 1959 and Holt 1970 for accounts of the Turkiyya and Mahdiyya; Gray 1961 and Collins 1962 for descriptions of nineteenth-century southern Sudan.

2. See Simonse 1992, 87–109, 306–8 for his analysis of the shifts in power from rain kings to cargo and warlord chiefs; Leonardi 2013a, 29–31 for a description of the same period in central Equatoria.

Chapter 6: The Dual Colonialism of the Condominium

1. Interview with Zahir Surur Asadat, secretary of the Retired Officers Club, Omdurman, 5 March 1980.

2. For details of military campaigns see Collins 1971; 1983.

3. "1930 Memorandum on Southern Policy" reprinted in Beshir 1968, 115–18 and Wai 1973, 175–79.

4. See Sanderson and Sanderson 1981 for a comprehensive history of educational policy in southern Sudan.

Chapter 7: The Politics of Competing Nationalisms

1. Minutes of the 1954 Liberal Conference in Wawa 2005, 115–37; Benjamin Lwoki to British Foreign Secretary in Johnson 1998c, 384–85, document 369; and Wawa 2005, 137–40.

Chapter 8: Two Wars

1. See http://www.goss.org/index.php/about-south-sudan/history (accessed 27 February 2015); Poggo 2009, 20. For an extended

comparison of the two civil wars see Johnson 2011b, from which parts of this chapter are extracted.

2. For more detailed descriptions of events surrounding the disturbances see Cotran 1956; Woodward 1979, 144–56; Johnson 1998c, 434–79, documents 392–419; Poggo 2009, chap. 2.

3. See Wakason 1984; Lagu 2006; and Poggo 2009 for detailed accounts of the Anyanya; Rolandsen 2011b for the beginnings of the Anyanya; Paterno 2007 for a life of Fr. Saturnino Lohure.

4. See LeRiche and Arnold 2012 for a military account of the second civil war.

Chapter 9: Self-Determination in the Twenty-First Century

1. This chapter is derived in part from Johnson 2013 published in *Civil Wars* 15, no. 2 on 25 August 2013, available online: http://www.tandfonline.com/doi/abs/10.1080/13698249.2013.817850.

2. Minutes of the 1947 Juba Conference quoted in Beshir 1968, 141; Wai 1973, 191; Wawa 2005, 53.

3. "Declaration on the Granting of Independence to Colonial Countries and Peoples," UN Res 1514(XV) of December 1960.

4. Author's notes on an address by John Garang, London, 2 March 2002.

5. Author's notes on an address by John Garang, London, 18 September 2004.

6. "Protocol between the Government of Sudan (GOS) and the Sudan People's Liberation Movement (SPLM) on the resolution of conflict in Southern Kordofan/Nuba Mountains and Blue Nile States," Naivasha, Kenya, 26 May 2004, clause 3.6.

Chapter 10: Legacies of War

1. A website, http://rememberingoneswelost.com, has been created to record all those killed in civil wars and disturbances since August 1955. As of July 2016, 4,649 deaths between December 2013 and August 2015 had been documented: 1,815 in Central Equatoria, 2,351 in Jonglei, 336 in Upper Nile, 129 in Unity, and 18 in Lakes. The numbers continue to rise.

Abbreviations and Glossary

Anyanya   (Moru/Madi) A poison derived from snake venom, the name adopted by southern Sudanese guerrillas during Sudan's first civil war (1962–72), sometimes retroactively referred to as Anyanya 1 to distinguish them from the Anyanya 2 insurgents who began a guerrilla war against the Khartoum government in the early 1980s.

Azande   A people of the Nile-Congo watershed. Azande (noun), Zande (adjective); thus the "Azande people," but "Zande kingdoms."

Baggara   (Ar.) Cattle-keeping Muslim Arab pastoralists in Darfur, Kordofan, and White Nile, including the Taa'isha and Rizeigat of Darfur, the Humr (Miseriyya) of Kordofan, and the Seleim of White Nile.

Bahr el-Ghazal   (Ar.) Name of a river and also of a province and region.

Condominium   The period of joint Anglo-Egyptian administration of Sudan (1899–1955).

CPA	Comprehensive Peace Agreement, signed in 2005, ending Sudan's second civil war.
DUP	Democratic Union Party, aligned with the Khatmiyya sect and the Mirghani family.
IGAD	Inter-governmental Authority for Development, the regional body including the governments of Sudan, Ethiopia, Eritrea, Kenya, and Uganda that coordinated the mediation leading to the CPA.
JAH	*Journal of African History.*
JEAS	*Journal of Eastern African Studies.*
jallaba	(Ar.) Petty trader, now used in South Sudan as a disparaging reference to northern Sudanese Arabs.
jihad	(Ar.) Literally to strive in the way of God, but more generally applied as war against unbelievers.
jihadiyya	(Ar.) Slave riflemen used in the Turco-Egyptian and Mahdist armies.
Mahdi	(Ar.) Muhammad Ahmad al-Mahdi (1848–1885), a Dongolawi carpenter and Sufi shaykh who proclaimed himself the Mahdi, the Expected One who would restore Islam to its original form. His movement expelled Egypt from Sudan, but he died shortly after capturing Khartoum and establishing the foundations of a theocratic state.

Mahdiyya	Period of the Mahdist revolution and theocratic state in Sudan (1881–98).
malakiyya	(Ar. sing., pl. *malakiyyat*) Referring to settlements or lineages of freed slaves and to civilian quarters of discharged soldiers in the main South Sudanese towns.
monyomiji	Age-class system adopted by many peoples in Eastern and Central Equatoria.
NCP	National Congress Party, successor to the NIF.
NIF	National Islamic Front.
NRO	National Records Office, Khartoum.
reth	(Shilluk) King; also *rwot* (Acholi), *rwath* (Pari).
SAF	Sudan Armed Forces.
SANU	Sudan African National Union, South Sudan's oldest political party, founded in 1962.
SIR	*Sudan Intelligence Report.*
SNR	*Sudan Notes and Records.*
SPLM/A	Sudan People's Liberation Movement/ Army, founded in 1983.
SSNA	South Sudan National Archive, Juba.
sudd	(Ar.) Literally obstruction or dam, the name applied to the central papyrus swamp on the Bahr el-Jebel.
Turkiyya	Period of Turco-Egyptian rule in Sudan (1820–85).

Umma	Umma Party, backed by the Ansar sect and led by the al-Mahdi family.
UNP	Upper Nile Province.
zariba	(Ar. sing., pl. *zara'ib*) Fortified camp.

Works Cited

Abdel-Rahim, M. 1969. *Imperialism and Nationalism in Sudan: A Study in Constitutional and Political Development, 1899–1956.* London: Oxford University Press.

Abu Hasabu, A. A. M. 1985. *Factional Conflict in the Sudanese Nationalist Movement, 1918–1948.* Khartoum: Graduate College Publications.

Adams, W. Y. 1977. *Nubia: Corridor to Africa.* London: Allen Lane.

African Union. 2014. "Final Report of the African Union Commission of Inquiry on South Sudan. Executive Summary." Addis-Abeba, 15 October. http://www.peaceau.org/uploads/auciss.executive.summary.pdf, accessed 27 October 2015.

Akol, J. 2005. *I Will Go the Distance.* Nairobi: Paulines Publications Africa.

Albino, O. 1970. *The Sudan: A Southern Viewpoint.* London: Oxford University.

Alier, A. 1990. *The Southern Sudan: Too Many Agreements Dishonoured.* Exeter: Ithaca Press.

Amnesty International. 2013. "'We Had No Time to Bury Them': War Crimes in Sudan's Blue Nile State." London: Amnesty International.

———. 2014. "Nowhere Safe: Civilians under Attack in South Sudan." London: Amnesty International.

———. 2015. "Sudan: Attacks in South Kordofan 'Constitute War Crimes.'" London: Amnesty International.

Angok, D. 2015. "Rainmaker Killed in Torit County." *Gurtong Trust,* http://www.gurtong.net/ECM/Editorial/tabid/124/ctl/ArticleView/mid/519/articleId/17187/categoryId/1/Rainmaker-Killed-in-Torit-County.aspx.

Anon. 1899. "Precis of News Received about Rabeh Zubehr Subsequent to the Date of the Memorandum, dated 19.12.98, Furnished to the Foreign Office (*Egypt December 21* Confidential Section 17)." NRO Intel 5/5/53.

Anon. 1965. "Sudan Mends Its Fences." *Africa Confidential,* August 13, 6.

Arkell, A. J. 1961. *A History of Sudan: From the Earliest Times to 1821.* London: Athlone Press.

Arop, A. M. 2006. *Sudan's Painful Road to Peace: A Full Story of the Founding and Development of SPLM/SPLA.* Book-Surge.

———. 2012. *The Genesis of Political Consciousness in South Sudan.* Charleston: no publisher.

Badal, R. K. 1986. "Oil and Regional Sentiment in the South." In *Sudan since Independence: Studies of the Political Development since 1956,* edited by M. Abd al-Rahim et al., 143–51. Aldershot: Gower.

———. 1994. "Political Cleavages within Southern Sudan: An Empirical Analysis of the Re-division Debate." In *Short-Cut to Decay: The Case of Sudan,* edited by S. Harir and T. Tvedt, 105–25. Uppsala: Nordiska Afrikainstituteet.

Badiey, N. 2014. *The State of Post-conflict Reconstruction: Land, Urban Development and State-building in Juba, Southern Sudan.* Woodbridge: James Currey.

Baer, G. 1967. "Slavery in Nineteenth Century Egypt." *JAH* 8, no. 3:417–41.

Baines, J. 1995. "Origins of Egyptian Kingship." In *Ancient Egyptian Kingship,* edited by D. O'Connor and D. P. Silvermann, 95–156. Leiden: Brill.

Balaton-Chrimes, S. 2011. "Citizens Minus: Rights, Recognition and Nubians of Kenya." PhD diss., Monash University, Australia.

Bartoli. 1970. "A History of the Sudan 1822–1841." In Hill 1970, 1–123.

Beaton, A. C. 1936. "The Bari: Clan and Age-Set System." *SNR* 19, no. 1:109–45.

Bedri, I. 1938. "Dinka Beliefs in Their Chiefs and Rainmakers." *SNR* 22, no. 1:125–31.

192

———. 1948. "More Notes on the Padang Dinka." *SNR* 29, no. 1:40–57.

Bermann, R. A. 1931. *The Mahdi of Allah: The Story of the Dervish Mohammed Ahmed.* London: Putnam.

Beshir, M. O. 1968. *The Southern Sudan: Background to Conflict.* London: C. Hurst.

Beswick, S. 2004. *Sudan's Blood Memory: The Legacy of War, Ethnicity, and Slavery in South Sudan.* Rochester: University of Rochester Press.

Bjørkelo, A. 1989. *Prelude to the Mahdiyya: Peasants and Traders in the Shendi Region, 1820–1885.* Cambridge: Cambridge University Press.

Bob, A-M. A., and S. S. Wassara. 1989. "The Emergence of the Organized Political Movement in Southern Sudan 1946–1972." In *The Nationalist Movement in the Sudan,* edited by M. A. Hag al Safi, 295–321. Khartoum: Institute of African and Asian Studies.

Bruce, J. 1790. *Travels to Discover the Source of the Nile in the Years 1768, 1769, 1770, 1771, 1772 and 1773,* vol. 4. Edinburgh: J. Ruthven.

Burton, J. W. 1987. *A Nilotic World: The Atuot-Speaking Peoples of the Southern Sudan.* Westport, CT: Greenwood Press.

Buxton, J. 1963. *Chiefs and Strangers: A Study of Political Assimilation among the Mandari.* Oxford: Clarendon Press.

———. 1973. *Religion and Healing in Mandari.* Oxford: Clarendon Press.

Colchester, T. C. 1950. "Bacchus Pasha." *Corona* 2, no. 1:39–40.

Cole, D. C., and R. Huntington. 1997. *Between a Swamp and a Hard Place: Development Challenges in Remote Rural Africa.* Cambridge, MA: Harvard Institute for International Development.

Collins, R. O. 1962. *The Southern Sudan, 1883–1898: A Struggle for Control.* New Haven: Yale University Press.

———. 1968. *King Leopold, England, and the Upper Nile, 1899–1909.* New Haven: Yale University Press.

———. 1971. *Land beyond the Rivers: The Southern Sudan, 1898–1918.* New Haven: Yale University Press.

————. 1983. *Shadows in the Grass: Britain in the Southern Sudan, 1918–1956.* New Haven: Yale University Press.

————. 1990. *The Waters of the Nile: Hydropolitics and the Jonglei Canal, 1900–1988.* Oxford: Oxford University Press.

Comyn, D. C. F. ff. 1911. *Service and Sport in the Sudan. A Record of Administration in the Anglo-Egyptian Sudan. With Some Intervals of Sport and Travel.* London: Bodley Head.

Coriat, P. 1993. *Governing the Nuer: Documents in Nuer History and Ethnography, 1922–31,* edited by D. H. Johnson. JASO Occasional Papers No. 9. Oxford: JASO.

Cormack, Z. T. 2014. "The Making and Remaking of Gogrial: Landscape, History and Memory in South Sudan." PhD diss., University of Durham.

Cotran, T. S. 1956. *Southern Sudan Disturbances August 1955: Report of the Commission of Enquiry.* Khartoum: McCorquedale.

Craze, J. 2014. "Contested Borders: Continuing Tensions over the Sudan–South Sudan Border." Geneva: Small Arms Survey.

Crazzolara, J. P. 1951. *The Lwoo. Part II, Lwoo Traditions.* Verona: Missioni Africane.

————. 1953. *Zur Gesellschaft und Religion der Nueer.* Vienna: Anthropos.

————. 1954. *The Lwoo. Part III, Clans.* Verona: Editrice Nigrizia.

Cunnison, I. 1966. *Baggara Arabs: Power and the Lineage in a Sudanese Nomad Tribe.* Oxford: Clarendon Press.

————. 1971. "Classification by Genealogy: A Problem of the Baqqara Belt." In *Sudan in Africa,* edited by Y. F. Hasan, 186–96. Khartoum: Khartoum University Press.

Daly, M. W. 1986. *Empire on the Nile: The Anglo-Egyptian Sudan, 1898–1934.* Cambridge: Cambridge University Press.

Danforth, J. C. 2002. "Report to the President of the United States on the Outlook for Peace in Sudan." http://www.state.gov/p/af/rls/rpt/2002/10150.htm.

David, N. 1982a. "The BIEA Southern Sudan Expedition of 1979: Interpretation of the Archaeological Data." In Mack and Robertshaw 1982, 49–57.

————. 1982b. "Prehistory and Historical Linguistics in Central Africa: Points of Contact." In *The Archaeological and*

Linguistic Reconstruction of African History, edited by C. Ehret and M. Posnansky, 78–95. Berkeley: University of California Press.

De Alessi, B. 2015. "Two Fronts, One War: Evolution of the Two Areas Conflict, 2014–15." Geneva: Small Arms Survey.

Dellagiacoma, Fr., ed. 1990. *How a Slave Became a Minister: Autobiography of Sayyed Stanislaus Abdallahi Paysama.* Khartoum: no publisher.

Deng, D. K. 2014a. "Memory, Healing and Transformation in South Sudan." Juba: South Sudan Law Society.

———. 2014b. "Truth and Dignity Commission: A Proposal to Reconcile the Many Truths of South Sudan from 1972 to the Present." Juba: South Sudan Law Society.

———. 2014c. "South Sudan Country Report. Findings of the Land Governance Assessment Framework (LGAF)." Juba: South Sudan Law Society.

———. 2015. "Large-Scale Land Investments in South Sudan." Juba: South Sudan Law Society.

Deng, F. M., ed. 1980. *Dinka Cosmology.* London: Ithaca Press.

———. 1986. *The Man Called Deng Majok. A Biography of Power, Polygyny, and Change.* New Haven: Yale University Press.

Deng, F. M., and M. W. Daly, eds. 1989. *Bonds of Silk: The Human Factor in the British Administration of the Sudan.* East Lansing: Michigan State University Press.

de Waal, A. 2014. "When Kleptocracy Becomes Insolvent: Brute Causes of the Civil War in South Sudan." *African Affairs* 113, no. 452:347–69.

Duffield, M. 1992. "Famine, Conflict and the Internationalization of Public Welfare." In *Beyond Conflict in the Horn: The Prospects for Peace, Recovery and Development in Ethiopia, Somalia, Eritrea and Sudan,* edited by M. Doornbos, L. Cliffe, A. G. M. Ahmed, and J. Markakis, 49–62. London: James Currey.

Edwards, D. N. 1998. "Meroe and the Sudanic Kingdoms." *JAH* 39, no. 2:175–93.

———. 2003. "Ancient Egypt in the Sudanese Middle Nile: A Case of Mistaken Identity?" In O'Connor and Reid 2003, 137–50.

Ehret, C. 1982. "Population Movement and Culture Contact in the Southern Sudan, c. 3000 BC to AD 1000: A Preliminary Linguistic Overview." In Mack and Robertshaw 1982, 19–48.

———. 2001a. "Sudanic Civilization." In *Agricultural and Pastoral Societies in Ancient and Classical History,* edited by Michael Adas, 224–74. Philadelphia: Temple University Press.

———. 2001b. *A Historical-Comparative Reconstruction of Nilo-Saharan.* Cologne: Rüdiger Köppe Verlag.

———. 2002. *The Civilizations of Africa: A History to 1800.* Charlottesville: University of Virginia Press.

El Sammani, M. O. 1984. *Jonglei Canal: Dynamics of Planned Change in the Twic Area.* Graduate College Publications Monograph 8. Khartoum: Khartoum University Press.

El-Tounsy, M. O. 1845. *Voyage au Darfour.* Paris: Benjamin Duprat.

Evans-Pritchard, E. E. 1931. "The Mberidi (Shilluk group) and Mbegumba (Basiri group) of the Bahr-el-Ghazal." *SNR* 14, no. 1:15–48.

———. 1932. "Ethnological Observations of Dar Fung." *SNR* 15, no. 1:1–61.

———. 1938. "Administrative Problems in the Southern Sudan." In *Oxford University Summer School on Colonial Administration, 1938,* edited by Margery Perham, 75–77. Oxford: Oxford University Press.

———. 1940a. *The Nuer.* Oxford: Clarendon Press.

———. 1940b. *The Political System of the Anuak of the Anglo-Egyptian Sudan.* London: Percy Lund Humphreys.

———. 1951. *Kinship and Marriage among the Nuer.* Oxford: Clarendon Press.

———. 1956. *Nuer Religion.* Oxford: Clarendon Press.

———. 1957. "Zande Border Raids." *Africa* 28, no. 3:217–31.

———. 1962. "Zande Kings and Princes." In E. E. Evans-Pritchard, *Essays in Social Anthropology,* 87–116. London: Faber and Faber.

———. 1971a. *The Azande: History and Political Institutions.* Oxford: Clarendon Press.

———. 1971b. "Sources, with Particular Reference to the Southern Sudan." *Cahiers d'études africaines* 11, no. 1:129–79.

Ewald, J. 1990. *Soldiers, Traders, and Slaves: State Formation and Economic Transformation in the Greater Nile Valley, 1700–1885*. Madison: University of Wisconsin Press.

Falge, C. 2016. *The Global Nuer: Transnational Life-Worlds, Religious Movements and War*. Cologne: Rüdiger Köppe Verlag.

Ferguson, R. B., and N. L. Whitehead. 2000. "The Violent Edge of Empire." In *War in the Tribal Zone: Expanding States and Indigenous Warfare*, edited by R. B. Ferguson and N. L. Whitehead, 1–30. 2nd ed. Santa Fe: School of American Research.

Feyissa, D. 2011. *Playing Different Games: The Paradox of Any-waa and Nuer Identification Strategies in the Gambella Region, Ethiopia*. New York: Berghahn.

Fuller, D. Q. 2003. "Pharonic or Sudanic? Models for Meroitic Society and Change." In O'Connor and Reid 2003, 169–84.

Garretson, P. P. 1986. "The Southern Sudan Welfare Committee and the 1947 Strike in the Southern Sudan." *Northeast African Studies* 8, nos. 2–3:181–91.

Grabska, K. 2014. *Gender, Home and Identity: Nuer Repatriation to South Sudan*. Woodbridge: James Currey.

Gray, R. 1961. *A History of the Southern Sudan, 1839–1889*. London: Oxford University Press.

———. 2002. "Some Reflections on Christian Involvement in the Conflict, 1955–1972." In *Religion and Conflict in Sudan*, edited by Y. F. Hasan and R. Gray, 114–25. Nairobi: Paulines Publications Africa.

Grover, J. N. 1946. "Handing Over Notes Pibor," 20–25 January. SSNA UNP 57.D.7.

al-Hajj, M. A. 1971. "Hayatu B. Sa'id: A Revolutionary Mahdist in the Western Sudan." In *Sudan in Africa*, edited by Y. F. Hasan, 128–41. Khartoum: Khartoum University Press.

Hallam, W. K. R. 1977. *The Life and Times of Rabih Fadl Allah*. Ilfracome: Arthur Stockwell.

Hansen, H. B. 1991. "Pre-colonial Immigrants and Colonial Servants: The Nubians in Uganda Revisited." *African Affairs* 90, no. 361:559–80.

Harvey, C. P. D. 1982. "The Archaeology of the Southern Sudan: Environmental Context." In Mack and Robertshaw 1982, 7–18.

Hassan, Y. F. 2002. "The Role of Religion in the North-South Conflict with Special Reference to Islam." In *Religion and Conflict in Sudan,* edited by Yusuf Fadl Hasan and Richard Gray, 23–47. Nairobi: Paulines Publications Africa.

Healy, S. 1983. "The Changing Idiom of Self-Determination in the Horn of Africa." In I. M. Lewis 1983, 93–109.

Henderson, K. D. D. 1939. "The Migration of the Messiria into South West Kordofan." *SNR* 22, no.1:49–77.

Henige, D. 1980. "'The Disease of Writing': Ganda and Nyoro Kinglists in a Newly-Literate World." In *The African Past Speaks,* edited by Joseph C. Miller, 240–61. Folkestone: Wm Dawson and Sons.

Hill, R. L. 1959. *Egypt in the Sudan, 1820–1881.* London: Oxford University Press.

———. 1967. *A Biographical Dictionary of the Sudan.* 2nd ed. London: Frank Cass.

———, ed. 1970. *On the Frontiers of Islam: The Sudan under Turco-Egyptian Rule, 1822–1845.* Oxford: Clarendon Press.

Hill, R. L., and P. Hogg. 1995. *A Black Corps d'Élite: An Egyptian Sudanese Conscript Battalion with the French Army in Mexico, 1863–1867, and Its Survivors in Subsequent African History.* East Lansing: Michigan State University Press.

Hofmayr, W. 1925. *Die Schilluk.* Vienna: Anthropos.

Holt, P. M. 1970. *The Mahdist State in the Sudan, 1881–1898.* 2nd ed. Oxford: Clarendon Press.

———. 1973. *Studies in the History of the Near East.* London: Frank Cass.

Howell, P. P. 1948. "'Pyramids' in the Upper Nile Region.' *Man* 48 no. 56:52–53.

———. 1953. "The Election and Installation of Reth Kur wad Fafiti of the Shilluk. With an Account of the Final Ceremonies by J. O. Udal." *SNR* 34, no. 2:189–203.

———. 1954. *A Manual of Nuer Law.* London: Oxford University Press for the International African Institute.

———. 1961. "Appendix to Chapter II." In Lienhardt 1961, 97–103.

Howell, P. P., M. Lock, and S. Cobb, eds. 1988. *The Jonglei Canal: Impact and Opportunity.* Cambridge: Cambridge University Press.

Howell, P. P., and W. P. G. Thompson. 1946. "The Death of the Reth of the Shilluk and the Installation of his Successor." *SNR* 27:5–85.

Hutchinson, S. 1995. *Nuer Dilemmas: Coping with Money, War, and the State, 1930–1992.* Los Angeles: University of California Press.

Ibrahim, F. N. 1991. "The Southern Sudanese Migration to Khartoum and the Resultant Conflicts." *GeoJournal* 25, no. 1:13–18.

Ibrahim, H. A. 1976. *The 1936 Anglo-Egyptian Treaty: An Historical Study with Special Reference to the Contemporary Situation in Egypt and the Sudan.* Khartoum: Khartoum University Press.

ICG. 2013a. *Sudan's Spreading Conflict (I): War in South Kordofan.* Africa Program Report no. 198. Brussels: International Crisis Group.

———. 2013b. *Sudan's Spreading Conflict (II): War in Blue Nile.* Africa Program Report no. 204. Brussels: International Crisis Group.

———. 2015. *Sudan and South Sudan's Merging Conflicts.* Africa Program Report no. 223. Brussels: International Crisis Group.

Jackson, H. C. 1970. *Black Ivory or the Story of El Zubeir Pasha, Slaver and Sultan, as told by Himself.* New York: Negro Universities Press reprint of 1913 Khartoum: Sudan Press edition.

Jackson, H. W. 1898. "Letter from Jackson Bey *re* Marchand's Dispositions, and Extracts from Fashoda Diary, 24 October to 7 November 1898." In *SIR* 60, 25th May to 31st December, Appendix 58a: 96–98.

Jal, G. G. 1987. "The History of the Jikany Nuer before 1920." PhD diss., School of Oriental and African Studies, London University.

———. 1989. *The Sudan Question in the Anglo-Egyptian Treaty of 1936: An Historical Study of Conflict in Anglo-Egyptian Relations in the Sudan, 1899–1936.* Juba: Juba University Press.

James, W. 1977. "The Funj Mystique: Approaches to a Problem of Sudan History." In *Text and Context,* edited by R. K. Jain, 95–133. Philadelphia: ISHI.

———. 1979.'*Kwanim Pa: The Making of the Uduk People. An Ethnographic Study of Survival in the Sudan-Ethiopian Borderlands.* Oxford: Clarendon Press.

———. 1988. *The Listening Ebony: Moral Knowledge, Religion, and Power among the Uduk of Sudan.* Oxford: Clarendon Press.

———. 2007. *War and Survival in Sudan's Frontierlands: Voices from the Blue Nile.* Oxford: Oxford University Press.

———. 2015. "Charles Jedrej and the 'Deep Rurals': A West African Model Moves to the Sudan, Ethiopia, and Beyond." *Critical African Studies.* Special Issue "Crossing Africa and Beyond: Essays in Honour of Marian Charles Jedrej (1943–2007)": 1–15, published online 1 May 2015.

James, W., G. Baumann, and D. H. Johnson, eds. 1996. *Juan Maria Schuver's Travels in North East Africa, 1880–1883.* London: Hakluyt Society.

Jedrej, M. C. 1995. *Ingessana: The Religious Institutions of a People of the Sudan-Ethiopia Borderland.* Leiden: Brill.

JEM [Justice and Equality Movement]. 2004. *The Black Book: Imbalance of Power and Wealth in Sudan.* English translation.

Johnson, D. H. 1981. "The Fighting Nuer: Primary Sources and the Origins of a Stereotype." *Africa* 51, no. 1:508–27.

———. 1982a. "Tribal Boundaries and Border Wars: Nuer–Dinka Relations in the Sobat and Zaraf Valleys, *c.*1860–1976." *JAH* 23, no. 2:183–203.

———. 1982b. "The Death of Gordon: A Victorian Myth." *Journal of Imperial and Commonwealth History* 10, no. 2:285–310.

———. 1986a. "Judicial Regulation and Administrative Control: Customary Law and the Nuer, 1898–1954." *JAH* 27, no. 1:59–78.

———. 1986b. "On the Nilotic Frontier: Imperial Ethiopia in the southern Sudan, 1898–1936." In *The Southern Marches of Imperial Ethiopia: Essays in History and Social Anthropology,* edited by D. L. Donham and W. James, 219–45. Cambridge: Cambridge University Press.

———. 1989a. "Political Ecology in the Upper Nile: The Twentieth Century Expansion of the Pastoral 'Common Economy.'" *JAH* 30, no. 3:89–117.

———. 1989b. "The Structure of a Legacy: Military Slavery in Northeast Africa." *Ethnohistory* 36, no. 1:72–88.

———. 1990. "Fixed Shrines and Spiritual Centres in the Upper Nile." *Azania* 25:41–56.

———. 1992. "Recruitment and Entrapment in Private Slave Armies: The Structure of the *Zara'ib* in the Southern Sudan." In *The Human Commodity, Perspectives on the Trans-Saharan Slave Trade,* edited by E. Savage, 162–73. London: Frank Cass.

———. 1993. "Prophecy and Mahdism in the Upper Nile: An Examination of Local Experiences of the Mahdiyya in the Southern Sudan." *British Journal of Middle Eastern Studies* 20, no. 1:42–56.

———. 1994. *Nuer Prophets.* Oxford: Clarendon Press.

———. 1995. "The Prophet Ngundeng and the Battle of Pading: Prophecy, Symbolism and Historical Evidence." In *Revealing Prophets: Prophecy in Eastern African History,* edited by D. M. Anderson and D. H. Johnson, 196–220. London: James Currey.

———. 1998a. "The Sudan People's Liberation Army and the Problem of Factionalism." In *African Guerrillas,* edited by C. Clapham, 53–72. Oxford: James Currey.

———, ed. 1998b. *Sudan, Part 1, 1942–1950.* British Documents on the End of Empire, Series B, vol. 5. London: Stationery Office.

———, ed. 1998c. *Sudan, Part 2, 1951–1956.* British Documents on the End of Empire, Series B, vol. 5. London: Stationery Office.

———. 2000a. "Conquest and Colonisation: Soldier Settlers in the Sudan and Uganda." *SNR* NS 4: 59–79.

————. 2000b. "Religion and Communal Conflict in the Sudan: The War against Paganism." *Bulletin of the Royal Institute for Inter-Faith Studies* 2, no. 2: 63–84.

————. 2007. "Political Intelligence, Colonial Ethnography and Analytical Anthropology in the Sudan." In *Ordering Africa: Anthropology, European Imperialism and the Politics of Knowledge,* edited by H. Tilley and R. Gordon, 309–35. Manchester: Manchester University Press.

————. 2008. "Why Abyei Matters: The Breaking Point of Sudan's Comprehensive Peace Agreement?" *African Affairs* 107, no. 426:1–19.

————. 2009a. "Tribe or Nationality? The Sudanese Diaspora and the Kenyan Nubis." *JEAS* 3 no. 1:112–31.

————. 2009b. "Decolonizing the Borders in Sudan: Ethnic Territories and National Development." In *Empire, Development and Colonialism: The Past in the Present,* edited by M. Duffield and V. Hewitt, 176–87. Woodbridge: James Currey.

————. 2009c. "The Nuer Civil Wars." In *Changing Identification and Alliances in North-East Africa,* vol. 2, edited by G. Schlee and E. E. Watson, 31–47. New York: Berghahn Books.

————. 2010. *When Boundaries Become Borders: The Impact of Boundary-Making in Southern Sudan's Frontier Zones.* London: Rift Valley Institute.

————. 2011a. *The Root Causes of Sudan's Civil Wars: Peace or Truce,* rev. ed. Woodbridge: James Currey.

————. 2011b. "Twentieth-Century Civil Wars." In *The Sudan Handbook,* edited by J. Ryle, J. Willis, S. Baldo, and J. M. Jok, 122–32. Woodbridge: James Currey for the Rift Valley Institute.

————. 2011c. "Abyei: Sudan's West Bank," http://www.enoughproject.org/publications/abyei-sudans-west-bank.

————. 2012. "The Heglig Oil Dispute between Sudan and South Sudan." *JEAS* 6, no. 3:561–69.

————. 2013. "New Sudan or South Sudan? The Multiple Meanings of Self-Determination in Sudan's Comprehensive Peace Agreement." *Civil Wars* 15, no. 2:141–56.

————. 2014. *Federalism in the History of South Sudanese Political Thought.* Rift Valley Institute Research Paper 1. London: Rift Valley Institute.

Johnson, D. H., and G. Prunier. 1993. "The Foundation and Expansion of the SPLA." In *The Civil War in the Sudan, 1983–1989,* edited by M. W. Daly and A. al-Awad, 117–41. London: British Academic Press.

Jok, J. M. 2001. *War and Slavery in Sudan.* Philadelphia: University of Pennsylvania Press.

Junker, W. 1890. *Travels in Africa during the Years 1875–1878.* London: Chapman and Hall.

———. 1891. *Travels in Africa during the Years 1879–1883.* London: Chapman and Hall.

Kasfir, N. 1977. "Southern Sudanese Politics since the Addis Ababa Agreement." *African Affairs* 76, no. 303:143–66.

Kibreab, G. 2002. *State Intervention and the Environment in Sudan, 1889–1989.* Lampeter: Edwin Mellen.

Kuendit, L. A. M. 2010. *The Dinka History: The Ancients of Sudan from Abuk and Garang at Creation to the Present Day Dinka.* Kampala: Mignic Technologies (U) Ltd.

Kurimoto, E. 1994. "Civil War and Regional Conflicts: The Pari and Their Neighbours in South-Eastern Sudan." In *Ethnicity and Conflict in the Horn of Africa,* edited by K. Fukui and J. Markakis, 94–111. London: James Currey.

———. 1995. "Trade Relations between Western Ethiopia and the Nile Valley during the Nineteenth Century." *Journal of Ethiopian Studies* 28, no. 1:53–68.

———. 1998. "Resonance of Age Systems in Southeastern Sudan." In *Conflict, Age and Power in North East Africa: Age Systems in Transition,* edited by E. Kurimoto and S. Simonse, 29–50. Oxford: James Currey.

Kurita, Y. 1989. "The Concept of Nationalism in the White Flag League Movement." In *The Nationalist Movement in the Sudan,* edited by M. A. Hag al Safi, 14–62. Khartoum: Institute of African and Asian Studies.

———. 1992. "The Role of the 'Negroid but Detribalized' People in the Sudanese Society 1920s—1940s." In *Second International Sudan Studies Conference Papers,* vol. 3:107–120. Durham: University of Durham.

———. 1997. *'Ali 'Abd al-Latif wa Thawra 1924* [Ali Abd al-Latif and the revolution of 1924]. Cairo: Sudanese Studies Centre.

Lagu, J. 2006. *Sudan: Odyssey through a State; From Ruin to Hope.* Omdurman: M.O.B. Center for Sudan Studies.

Lako, G. T. 1985. "The Impact of the Jonglei Scheme on the Economy of the Dinka." *African Affairs* 84, no. 333:15–38.

Lamothe, R. M. 2011. *Slaves of Fortune: Sudanese Soldiers in the River War, 1896–1898.* Woodbridge: James Currey.

Large, D., and L. Patey. 2011. *Sudan Looks East: China, India and the Politics of Asian Alternatives.* Woodbridge: James Currey.

Leonardi, C. 2007. "'Liberation' or Capture: Youth in between 'Hakuma' and 'Home' during Civil War and Its Aftermath in Southern Sudan." *African Affairs* 106, no. 204:391–412.

———. 2013a. *Dealing with Government in South Sudan: Making Histories of Chiefship, Community and State.* Woodbridge: James Currey.

———. 2013b. "South Sudanese Arabic and the Negotiation of the Local State, *c.* 1840–2011." *JAH* 54, no. 3:351–72.

Leopold, M. 2005. *Inside West Nile: Violence, History and Representation on an African Frontier.* Oxford: James Currey.

———. 2007. "Legacy of Slavery in North West Uganda: The Story of the 'One-Elevens.'" In *Slavery in the Great Lakes Region of East Africa,* edited by H. Médard and S. Doyle, 124–44. Oxford: James Currey.

LeRiche, M., and M. Arnold. 2012. *South Sudan: From Revolution to Independence.* London: Hurst.

Lewis, B. A. 1972. *The Murle: Red Chiefs and Black Commoners.* Oxford: Clarendon Press.

Lewis, I. M., ed. 1983. *Nationalism and Self Determination in the Horn of Africa.* London: Ithaca Press.

Lienhardt, R. G. 1955. "Nilotic Kings and their Mothers' Kin." *Africa* 25:29–42.

———. 1958. "The Western Dinka." In *Tribes without Rulers,* edited by J. Middleton and D. Tait, 97–135. London: Routledge and Kegan Paul.

———. 1961. *Divinity and Experience. The Religion of the Dinka.* Oxford: Clarendon Press.

———. 1975. "Getting Your Own Back: Themes in Nilotic Myth." In *Studies in Social Anthropology. Essays in Memory of Evans-Pritchard by His Former Oxford Colleagues,* edited by J. H. M. Beattie and R. G. Lienhardt, 213–37. Oxford: Clarendon Press.

Luffin, X. 2013. "Kinubi." In *The Survey of Pidgin and Creole Languages,* vol. 3, edited by S. M. Michaelis et al., 50–53. Oxford: Oxford University Press.

———. 2014. "The Influence of Swahili on Kinubi." *Journal of Pidgin and Creole Languages* 29, no. 2:299–318.

Lwoki, B. 1954. Letter to Foreign Secretary, reprinted in Johnson 1998c, 384–85 as document 369; and in Wawa 2005, 137–40.

Lwong, J. 2013. "The Installation of the Shilluk (King) Reth," http://pachodo.org/latest-news-articles/community-news/530-the-installation-of-the-shilluk-king-reth.

Lyth, R. E. 1954. "Handing Over Notes on Akobo Town," 16 June. SSNA UNP 57.D.7.

Machell, P. 1896. "Memoirs of a Soudanese Soldier (Ali Effendi Gifoon)." *Cornhill Magazine,* NS 1, no. 440:175–87.

Mack, J., and P. Robertshaw, eds. 1982. *Culture History in the Southern Sudan: Archaeology, Linguistics, Ethnohistory.* Memoir No. 8 of the British Institute in Eastern Africa. Nairobi: British Institute in Eastern Africa.

Mahmud, U. A. 1983. *Arabic in the Southern Sudan: History and Spread of a Pidgin Creole.* Khartoum: FAL Advertising and Printing.

Makris, G. 2000. *Changing Masters: Spirit Possession and Identity Construction among Slave Descendants and Other Subordinates in the Sudan.* Evanston: Northwestern University Press.

Manfredi, S., and S. Petrollino. 2013. "Juba Arabic." In *The Survey of Pidgin and Creole Languages,* vol. 3, edited by S. M. Michaelis et al., 54–65. Oxford: Oxford University Press.

Marno, E. 1873. "Der Bahr Seraf." *Petermann's Mitteilungen* 19: 130–36.

Mawson, A. N. M. 1989. "The Triumph of Life: Political Disputes and Religious Ceremonial among the Agar Dinka of the Southern Sudan." PhD diss., Cambridge University.

————. 1991. "Murahaleen Raids on the Dinka, 1985–89." *Disasters* 15, no. 2:137–49.

Mawut, L. L. 1983. *Dinka Resistance to Condominium Rule, 1902–1932.* Khartoum: Graduate College Publications.

Mayall, J. 1983. "Self-Determination and the OAU." In Lewis 1983, 77–82.

Mayom, E. K. 1957. "The Political and Administrative Principles for the Southern Sudan." In Wawa 2005, 150–55.

Meldon, J. A. 1908. "Notes on the Sudanese in Uganda." *Journal of the Africa Society* 7, no. 26:123–46.

————. 1913. "English-Arabic Dictionary of Words and Phrases Used by the Sudanese in Uganda." School of Oriental and African Studies Library, Ms. 53704.

Mercer, P. 1971. "Shilluk Trade and Politics, from the Mid-Seventeenth Century to 1861." *JAH* 12, no. 3:407–26.

Moro, L. M. 2008. "Oil, Conflict and Displacement in Sudan." DPhil diss., University of Oxford.

Nakao, S. 2013. "A History from Below: Malakia in Juba, South Sudan, c.1927–1954." *Journal of Sophia Asian Studies* 31:139–60.

Nhial, A. A. J. 1975. "Kinubi and Juba Arabic: a Comparative Study." In *Directions in Sudanese Linguistics and Folklore,* edited by S. Hurreiz and H. Bell, 81–94. Khartoum: Institute of African and Asian Studies.

Niblock, T. 1987. *Class and Power in Sudan: The Dynamics of Sudanese Politics, 1898–1985.* London: Macmillan.

Nyaba, P. A. 2011. *South Sudan: The State We Aspire To.* Cape Town: Centre for Advanced Study of African Society.

O'Connor, D., and A. Reid, eds. 2003. *Ancient Egypt in Africa.* London: UCL Press.

Oduho, J., and W. Deng. 1963. *The Problem of the Southern Sudan.* London: Oxford University Press.

O'Fahey, R. S. 1980. *State and Society in Dar Fur.* London: C. Hurst.

————. 1982. "Fur and Fartit: The History of a Frontier." In Mack and Robertshaw 1982, 75–87.

O'Fahey, R. S., and J. L. Spaulding. 1974. *Kingdoms of the Sudan.* London: Methuen.

Ogot, B. A. 1967. *History of the Southern Luo,* vol. 1: *Migration and Settlement.* Nairobi: East African Publishing House.

OHCHR [Office of the High Commissioner for Human Rights]. 2015. "Report on the Human Rights Situation in South Sudan." Advance Unedited Version, A/HRC/28/49. United Nations High Commissioner for Human Rights.

Parliament of the Sudan. 1954. *2nd Session of the First Parliament, Weekly Digest of the House of Representatives* no. 6, 19th–22nd April.

Parsons, T. 1997. "'Kibera Is Our Blood': The Sudanese Military Legacy in Nairobi's Kibera Location, 1902–1968." *International Journal of African Historical Studies* 30, no. 1:87–122.

PASS. 2010. "Communiqué Dinka Malual & Rezeigat [*sic*] Grassroots Peace Conference, January 22nd to 25th 2010." Aweil: Northern Bahr el-Ghazal State.

Paterno, S. A. 2007. *The Rev. Fr. Saturnino Lohure: A Roman Catholic Priest Turned Rebel, the South Sudan Experience.* Baltimore: Publish America.

Petherick, Mr. and Mrs. J. 1869. *Travels in Central Africa,* vol. 1. London: Tinsley Bros.

Pinaud, C. 2013. "Women, Guns and Cattle: A Social History of the Second Civil War in South Sudan." PhD diss., Université Paris 1 Panthéon-Sorbonne.

Poggo, S. S. 2009. *The First Sudanese Civil War: Africans, Arabs and Israelis in the Southern Sudan, 1955–1972.* New York: Palgrave Macmillan.

Pumphrey, M. E. C. 1941. "The Shilluk Tribe." *SNR* 24:1–46.

Purvis, A. 1993. "'When the flyers from heaven stop, we will die.'" *Time,* April 12, 46–47.

Reining, C. 1966. *The Zande Scheme.* Evanston: Northwestern University Press.

Robertson, J. W. 1974. *Transition in Africa.* London: C. Hurst.

Rolandsen, Ø. H. 2010. "Civil War Society? Political Processes, Social Groups and Conflict Intensity in the Southern Sudan, 1955–2005." PhD diss., University of Oslo.

———. 2011a. "A False Start: Between War and Peace in the Southern Sudan, 1956–62." *JAH* 52, no. 1:108–11.

————. 2011b. "The Making of the Anya-Nya Insurgency in the Southern Sudan, 1961–64." *JEAS* 5, no. 2:211–32.

Rone, J. 2003. *Sudan, Oil, and Human Rights Abuses.* Washington, DC: Human Rights Watch.

Rottenburg, R., G. K. Komey, and E. Ille. 2011. *The Genesis of Recurring Wars in Sudan: Rethinking the Violent Conflicts in the Nuba Mountains/South Kordofan.* Halle: University of Halle.

Sanderson, L. P., and N. Sanderson. 1981. *Education, Religion and Politics in Southern Sudan 1899–1964.* London: Ithaca Press.

Santandrea, S. 1964. *A Tribal History of the Western Bahr el Ghazal.* Bologna: Editrice Nigrizia.

————. 1968. *The Luo of the Bahr el Ghazal.* Bologna: Editrice Nigrizia.

Santschi, M. 2009. *Report: Dinka Malual—Misseryia Peace Conference, 11–14 November, Aweil, South Sudan.* Bern: Swisspeace.

SANU. 1963. "Letter from SANU to African Liberation Committee," 5 December, reprinted in Wawa 2005, 171–78.

Schomerus, M., and T. Allen. 2010. *Southern Sudan at Odds with Itself: Dynamics of Conflict and Predicaments of Peace.* London: DESTIN.

Schweinfurth, G. 1874a. *The Heart of Africa,* vol. 1. New York: Harper and Brothers.

————. 1874b. *The Heart of Africa,* vol. 2. New York: Harper and Brothers.

SDIT [Southern Development Investigation Team]. 1955. *Natural Resources and Development Potential in the Southern Provinces of the Sudan. A Preliminary Report by the Southern Development Investigation Team, 1954.* London: Sudan Government.

SHRM. 2011. *Sudan Human Rights Monitor April–May 2011.* New York: African Centre for Justice and Peace Studies.

Sikainga, A. A. 1983. *The Western Bahr al-Ghazal under British Rule.* Athens: Ohio University Press.

————. 2000. "Military Slavery and the Emergence of a Southern Sudanese Diaspora in the Northern Sudan, 1884–1954."

In *White Nile, Black Blood: War, Leadership and Ethnicity from Kampala to Khartoum,* edited by J. Spaulding and S. Beswick, 23–37. Lawrenceville: Red Sea Press.

———. 2014. *Slaves into Workers: Emancipation and Labor in Colonial Sudan.* Austin: University of Texas Press.

Simonse, S. 1992. *Kings of Disaster: Dualism, Centralism and the Scapegoat King in Southeastern Sudan.* Leiden: E. J. Brill.

———. 1998. "Age, Conflict and Power in the *Monyomiji* Age Systems." In *Conflict, Age and Power in North East Africa: Age Systems in Transition,* edited by E. Kurimoto and S. Simonse, 51–78. Oxford: James Currey.

Soghayroun, I. E. 1981. *The Sudanese Muslim Factor in Uganda.* Khartoum: Khartoum University Press.

Spaulding, J. 1982. "Slavery, Land Tenure and Social Class in the Northern Turkish Sudan." *International Journal of African Historical Studies* 15, no. 1:1–20.

SPLM. 1983. *Sudan People's Liberation Movement Manifesto.*

———. 1992. "Opening Address to the Abuja Peace Talks," 26 May.

SPLM/SPLA. 1992. "Joint Abuja Delegation Declaration," 1 June.

SSHRC [South Sudan Human Rights Commission]. 2014. "Interim Report on South Sudan Internal Conflict December 15, 2013–March 15, 2014."

SSLM. 1972. "The South Sudan Liberation Movement Recommendations for a New Constitution for the Republic of the Sudan," 15 February.

SSLS [South Sudan Law Society]. 2015. "Summary Findings of the Perception Survey on Truth, Justice, Reconciliation and Healing in South Sudan." Juba: Access to Justice and Rule of Law Project.

Steevens, G. W. 1898. *With Kitchener to Khartum.* Edinburgh: William Blackwood.

Stigand, C. H. 1917. "Report on the Installation of the Mek Fafidi." SSNA UNP GO 40–43.

Stringham, N. 2016. "Marking Nuer Histories: Gender, Gerontocracy, and the Politics of Incorporation in South Sudan from 1400—1935." PhD diss., University of Virginia.

Taylor, B. 1970. *A Journal to Central Africa.* New York: Negro Universities Press reprint of 1854 edition.

Thomas, E. 2010. *The Kafia Kingi Enclave: People, Politics and History in the North-South Boundary of Western Sudan.* London: Rift Valley Institute.

————. 2014. *South Sudan: A Slow Liberation.* London: Zed Books.

Thuriaux-Hennebert, A. 1964. *Les Zande dans l'histoire du Bahr el Ghazal et de l'Equatoria.* Brussels: Institute de sociologie de l'Université libre.

Tounsel, C. 2015. "The Construction of Religious Nationalism in Southern Sudan, 1898–2011." PhD diss., University of Michigan.

Trigger, B. 1976. *Nubia under the Pharoahs.* Boulder: Westview Press.

Tucker, A. N. 1931. "The Tribal Confusion around Wau." *SNR* 14, no. 1:49–60.

Tunnicliffe, E. C. 1933. "Handing Over Notes," November. SSNA UNP 57.D.7.

Tuttle, B. R. 2014. "Life Is Prickly: Narrating History, Belonging and Common Place in Bor, South Sudan." PhD diss., Temple University.

UNHRC. 2016. *Assessment Mission by the Office of the United Nations High Commissioner for Human Rights to Improve Human Rights, Accountability, Reconciliation and Capacity in South Sudan: Detailed Findings,* A/HRC/31/49.

UNMIS. 2011. *Report on the Human Rights Situation during the Violence in Southern Kordofan, Sudan.* Khartoum: UNMIS Human Rights Section.

UNMISS. 2014a. "Interim Report on Human Rights Crisis in South Sudan. Report Coverage 15 December 2013–31 January 2014." United Nation Mission in the Republic of South Sudan Human Rights Division, 21 February.

————. 2014b. "Conflict in South Sudan. A Human Rights Report." United Nations Mission in the Republic of South Sudan, 8 May.

————. 2014c. "Special Report: Attack on Bentiu, Unity State, 29 October 2014." United Nations Mission in the Republic of South Sudan, 19 December.

———. 2015. "Flash Human Rights Report on the Escalation of Fighting in Greater Upper Nile. April/May 2015." United Nations Mission in the Republic of South Sudan, 29 June.

Vaughan, C. 2013. "The Rizeigat-Malual Borderland during the Condominium: The Limits of Legibility." In C. Vaughan, M. Schomerus, and L. de Vries 2013, 133–52.

Vaughan, C., M. Schomerus, and L. de Vries, eds. 2013. *The Borderlands of South Sudan: Authority and Identity in Contemporary and Historical Perspectives.* New York: Palgrave Macmillan.

Vezzadini, E. 2015. *Lost Nationalism: Memory, Insurgency, and Revolutionary Departures in Colonial Sudan.* Woodbridge: James Currey.

Wai, D. M., ed. 1973. *The Southern Sudan: The Problem of National Integration.* London: Frank Cass.

Wakason, E. N. 1984. "The Origin and Development of the Anya-Nya Movement, 1955–1972." In *Southern Sudan: Regionalism and Religion,* edited by Mohamed Omer Beshir, 127–204. Khartoum: Graduate College Publication No. 10.

———. 1993. "The Politics of Southern Self-Government, 1972–83." In *Civil War in the Sudan,* edited by M. W. Daly and A. A. Sikainga, 27–50. London: British Academic Press.

Walz, T. 1985. "Black Slavery in Egypt during the Nineteenth Century as Reflected in the Mahkama Archives of Cairo." In *Slaves and Slavery in Muslim Africa,* vol. 2: *The Servile Estate,* edited by J. R. Willis, 137–60. London: Frank Cass.

Wawa, Y., ed. 2005. *Southern Sudanese Pursuits of Self-Determination: Documents in Political History.* Kisubi: Marianum Press.

Welsby, D. A. 1996. *The Kingdom of Kush: The Napatan and Meroitic Empires.* London: British Museum Press.

Wengrow, D. 2003. "Landscapes of Knowledge, Idioms of Power: The African Foundations of Ancient Egyptian Civilization Reconsidered." In O'Connor and Reid 2003, 121–35.

———. 2006. *The Archaeology of Early Egypt: Social Transformations in North-East Africa, 10,000 to 2650 BC.* Cambridge: Cambridge University Press.

—————. 2010. *What Makes Civilization? The Ancient Near East and the Future of the West.* Oxford: Oxford University Press.

Wengrow, D., M. Dee, S. Foster, A. Stevenson, and C. B. Ramsey. 2014. "Cultural Convergence in the Neolithic of the Nile Valley: A Prehistoric Perspective on Egypt's Place in Africa." *Antiquity* 88:95–11.

Westermann, D. 1970. *The Shilluk People: Their Language and Folklore.* Westport: Negro Universities Press reprint of the 1912 edition.

Wiberg, H. 1983. "Self-Determination as an International Issue." In Lewis 1983, 43–65.

Williams, B. B. 1997. "The Wearer of the Leopard Skin in the Naqada Period." In *Ancient Egypt, the Aegean, and the Near East: Studies in Honour of Martha Rhoads Bell,* edited by J. Phillips, 483–96. San Antonio: Van Siclen Books.

Willis, C. A. 1995. *The Upper Nile Province Handbook: A Report on Peoples and Government in the Southern Sudan, 1931,* edited by D. H. Johnson. Oxford: Oxford University Press for the British Academy. 2015 paperback reprint Wanneroo, WA: Africa World Books.

Willis, J. 2002. *Potent Brews: A Social History of Alcohol in East Africa 1850–1999.* Oxford: James Currey/Ohio University Press.

Wilson, S. C. 1901. *"Jehovah-Nissi." The Life Story of Hatashil-Masha-Kathish.* Birmingham: C. Caswell.

—————. c.1939. *I Was a Slave.* London: Stanley Paul.

Winter, R. K. 1933. "Address by the Chairman, R.K. Winter, Secretary for Education and Health. Record of Proceedings at an Educational Conference held at Juba on April 1st, 3rd and 4th, 1933." SSNA, UNP SCR 17.A.2 vol. II.

Woodward, P. 1979. *Condominium and Sudanese Nationalism.* London: Rex Collings.

Wright, M. 1993. *Strategies of Slaves and Women: Life-Stories from East/Central Africa.* New York: Lilian Barber Press.

Wynne-Jones, R. 2012. "Cymbeline: From War-Ravaged South Sudan to the Globe Theatre." *Independent,* May 2, www .independent.co.uk/arts-entertainment/theatre-dance

/features/cymbeline-from-warravaged-south-sudan-to
-the-globe-theatre-7704215.html.

Young, J. 2012. *The Fate of Sudan: The Origins and Consequences of a Flawed Peace Process.* London: Zed Books.

———. 2015. "A Fractious Rebellion: Inside the SPLM-IO."
Geneva: Small Arms Survey.

.

Acknowledgments

This book emerges from nearly fifty years' research in South Sudan's history, and there are more persons to be thanked than there is space to thank them. My foremost acknowledgement must be to my wife, Wendy James, to whom this book is dedicated. We have been in a lifelong conversation about the history and ethnography of the Nile Basin, and she has ensured that my historical horizon has not been completely bounded by South Sudan's present borders. Numerous South Sudanese have stimulated my interest in their history, from my classmates at (then) Makerere University College to fellow toilers in today's revived South Sudan National Archive. A special thanks goes to my friend and former colleague in the Southern Regional Ministry of Culture and Information, Atem Yaak Atem, who, as the editor of *Southern Sudan* magazine and *The Pioneer,* invited me to write columns on South Sudanese history. The development of my understanding of how to study South Sudan's past owes much to my teachers. First Wyatt MacGaffey, Harvey Glickman, Rob Mortimer, and John Spielman at Haverford College; then my UCLA supervisors Terry Ranger and Chris Ehret; and finally my informal tutors in Oxford, Godfrey and Peter Lienhardt. Participation in the Rift Valley Institute's projects has brought me in close touch with a new generation of researchers, among them Eddie Thomas, who gave me a detailed set of comments on this manuscript and suggestions, some of which I have followed. Overdue thanks are owed my long-suffering friend Peter Garretson for giving me a base in Khartoum in between bouts of fieldwork, malaria, and hepatitis. Finally my thanks to Gill Berchowitz, former publishing colleague, sometime poetic muse, patient editor, and still good friend, who originally proposed this book and has seen it through to publication.

Index

Azande, 54, 84, 122, 187; in
    armies, 71, 84, 86; kingdoms,
    54–55, 69–71; language, 32,
    55; military campaign against,
    104; mixed population, 55,
    76, 79, 81
Azande kings, 24–25, 54, 71,
    73, 103, 108; King Ndoruma
    Ezo, 74–75, 104; King
    Tambura Liwa, 74–75, 82,
    104; King Tikima, 70; King
    Yambio Bazingbi (Gbudwe),
    74–75, 104

Baggara, 43, 61, 62, 64, 77, 84,
    172, 182, 187; Humr, 56, 70,
    88, 187; Misseriya, 141, 182,
    187; Rizeigat, 56, 70, 82, 111,
    171, 182, 187; Seleim, 110–11,
    187; Ta'aishi, 85, 187
Bahr el-Ghazal, 187; dialect
    of Arabic spoken in, 94; in
    nineteenth century, 69–71,
    75, 81–82, 84–86; peoples
    of, 45, 57, 84, 111, 122, 182;
    political leaders from, 131;
    province, 25, 33, 95, 104–5,
    107; river basin, 31, 34, 55–56;
    in wartime, 129, 133, 145;
    western Bahr el-Ghazal, 55,
    61, 64, 105, 110, 171
Bari, 34, 50, 65; age-sets, 51; clans,
    49, 54; language, 21, 31–32;
    myths, 46; warlords, 66–67
Bari kings and chiefs, 65–67, 106,
    122; Bepo-lo-Nyiggilo, 66;
    Laku-lo-Rundiyang, 65–66;
    Logunu, 65; Loro-lo-Laku,
    65–66; Nyiggilo, 65; Subek
    (Jubek), 65
Blue Nile, 24, 31, 50, 55, 88;
    foothills, 78; peoples of, 125,
    153, 158; province, 111, 151;
    river, 47, 52; and SPLM/A,
    142, 144, 146, 149, 170;
    struggle for land in, 158–59

cattle, 35–37, 178–79; and
    administration, 102, 104;
    Apis Bull, 37–38; bovine
    idiom, 36; cattle burials,
    36–37; color symbolism of,
    38; in patronage, 174; primary
    pastoral communities, 36, 47;
    Tutgar, 38; and zariba system,
    69, 72, 82. *See also* Baggara
chiefs, 42; in Anglo-Egyptian
    administration, 102, 105–9,
    113; cargo chiefs, 65–66,
    106; definition of, 22; and
    education, 122; at Juba
    Conferences, 120, 125; sacral
    chiefs, 40–41; trading chiefs,
    67; warlord chiefs, 66
civil wars, 134; 1955
    Disturbances, 135–36; first
    civil war (1962–72), 137–49;
    influence of Cold War, 139–
    40; massacres during, 139;
    mutinies preceding, 140–41;
    religion and, 147–48; revenge
    killings, 179; second civil war
    (1989–2005), 140–6; in South
    Sudan (post-2013), 175–76,
    179–81; Torit Mutiny, 125
clan, definition of, 19–20
Comprehensive Peace Agreement
    (CPA), 98, 134, 163–64, 169,
    181, 188; boundaries, 171;
    Government of National
    Unity (GoNU), 164; interim
    period, 173; Machakos
    Protocol, 146, 160; popular
    consultations, 149, 161–62,
    165–66; security protocol,
    145–46

Darfur, 95, 130, 151; army of,
    61; borderlands with Bahr
    el-Ghazal, 84, 110–11, 172;
    conquered by Zubair Pasha,
    70, 84; peoples of, 31, 187;
    slave-raiding state, 55, 60, 62,

Garang, John, 16, 144, 156, 166, 186nn9:4–5; answers critics, 161–62; anti-Garang forces, 145; cofounder of SPLM/A, 141; death of, 173; sworn in as First Vice President, 98

Hamites, 21

independence referendum, 28, 111, 119, 166–67; referendum law, 164

Inter-governmental Authority for Development (IGAD), 188; negotiations in Addis Ababa, 180; peace talks, 145–46, 157, 159–60

Islamic state/law, 132, 133, 143, 149, 160

isolation of South Sudan, 18–19, 41

Juba Conferences: 1947 conference, 116–18, 120, 123, 124, 152, 154, 186n9:2; 1954 conference, 125, 126, 153, 185n7:1

Kenya, 15, 20, 31, 48–49, 184; border with South Sudan, 16; hosts peace talks, 146, 188; southern Sudanese in, 88, 92–93, 182

Kiir Mayardit, Salva, 141, 173

kingship/kings/kingdoms, 22, 51, 53; in Equatoria, 54; Nilotic, 46, 79; rainmaker kings, 41, 54, 64; sacral kingship, 35–36, 40–41, 53–54. See also Anuak; Azande kings; Bari kings and chiefs; Shilluk kings

languages, 31–32; Arabic, 78, 94, 102, 106–8, 109, 183; Juba Arabic, 93–94, 168; Ki-Nubi, 93–94; Koman, 44, 50, 53; Nilo-Hamitic, 21; Sudanic, 34, 51–52, 55; vernaculars, 107–8,

113. See also Nilo-Saharan; Nilotic

Lotuho, 20, 21, 34; age-sets, 51; dissident rain king, 137; military campaign against, 105; trade with, 65

Luo, 32, 34, 41, 50, 53; in eastern Africa, 48–49; Jo-Luo, 45; Shilluk-Luo, 82

Mahdiyya/Mahdists, 60, 72, 104, 106, 185n4:1, 189; invasion of Egypt, 95; Mahdist state, 83, 85, 88, 94; in southern Sudan, 58, 66–69, 75, 76, 82, 99, 107, 121

missionaries: Church Missionary Society, 122; J. P. Crazzolara, 23, 48; expelled, 147; W. Hofmayr, 23; mission education, 122; missionary societies, 113; S. Santandrea, 23

myths and legends: rope to the sky, 44; spear and bead, 46–47; trees, 42–45; wandering bulls, 47–48

nationalism: 1924 rising, 97; African, 148; Arabization, 136–37; Egyptian, 96, 114, 118; pan-Arabism, 28, 127, 136; Society of the Sudanese Union, 96–97; Sudanese, 28, 114, 118, 121

neighboring peoples: Fur, 31–32, 122, 125, 151; Ingessana, 31, 111, 151; Turkana, 21; Uduk, 44–45, 50, 111. See also Baggara; Nuba

new men and women, 67–68, 71, 76, 79, 81, 106–7; Achol (Dinka trader), 72; Bakhit Bey Batraki (Nuba governor), 72; Deng Cier, 73; Faragalla Buluk Amin (Cany Reth), 107; Faragalla

221